Report to the Commissioner of Internal Revenue

I0426308

June 2012

INTERNAL REVENUE SERVICE

Status of GAO Financial Audit and Related Financial Management Recommendations

GAO

Accountability * Integrity * Reliability

GAO-12-695

June 2012

INTERNAL REVENUE SERVICE

Status of GAO Financial Audit and Related Financial Management Recommendations

Why GAO Did This Study

In its role as the nation's tax collector, IRS has a demanding responsibility to annually collect trillions of dollars in taxes, process hundreds of millions of tax and information returns, and enforce the nation's tax laws.

Each year, as part of the annual audit of IRS's financial statements, GAO makes recommendations to address control deficiencies identified during the audit and follows up on the status of IRS's efforts to address the control deficiencies GAO identified in previous years' audits. The purpose of this report is to (1) provide an overview of the financial management challenges still facing IRS, (2) provide the status of financial audit–related recommendations and the actions needed to address them, and (3) highlight the relationship between GAO's recommendations and internal control activities central to IRS's mission and goals.

What GAO Recommends

GAO is not making any recommendations in this report. In commenting on a draft of this report, the IRS Commissioner stated that the agency is committed to implementing appropriate improvements to maintain sound financial management practices.

View GAO-12-695. For more information, contact Steven J. Sebastian at (202) 512-3406 or sebastians@gao.gov

What GAO Found

The Internal Revenue Service (IRS) has made significant progress in improving its internal controls and financial management since its first financial statement audit in 1992, as evidenced by 12 consecutive years of clean audit opinions on its financial statements, the resolution of several material control deficiencies, and actions resulting in the closure of over 300 financial management recommendations. This progress has been the result of hard work throughout IRS and sustained commitment at the top levels of the agency. However, IRS still faces significant financial management challenges in (1) resolving its remaining material weaknesses and significant deficiency in internal control, (2) developing outcome-oriented performance metrics, and (3) correcting numerous other control deficiencies, especially those relating to safeguarding tax receipts and taxpayer information. At the beginning of GAO's audit of IRS's fiscal year 2011 financial statements, 77 recommendations from prior audits remained open because IRS had not fully addressed the underlying issues. During the fiscal year 2011 financial audit, IRS took actions that GAO considered sufficient to close 38 recommendations. At the same time, GAO identified additional control deficiencies resulting in 30 new recommendations. In total, 69 recommendations remain open. GAO has also identified numerous control deficiencies and made recommendations related to information security that have been reported separately and are not included in this report because of the sensitive nature of many of those control deficiencies.

To assist IRS in evaluating and improving internal controls, GAO categorized the 69 open recommendations by various internal control activities, which, in turn, were grouped into three broad control categories.

Summary of Recommendations Grouped by Control Category				
	Open at the beginning of 2011	Closed during 2011 audit	New from 2011 audit	Total remaining open
Safeguarding of assets and security activities	29	12	1	18
Proper recording and documenting of transactions	30	18	17	29
Effective management review and oversight	18	8	12	22
Total	77	38	30	69

Source: GAO.

The continued existence of control deficiencies that gave rise to these recommendations represents a serious challenge for IRS. Effective implementation of GAO's recommendations could greatly assist IRS in improving its internal controls and achieving sound financial management, which are integral to effectively carrying out its tax administration responsibilities.

Contents

Abbreviations

CFO	Chief Financial Officer
FMFIA	Federal Managers' Financial Integrity Act of 1982
FTHBC	First-time Homebuyer Credit
IRM	Internal Revenue Manual
IRS	Internal Revenue Service
OMB	Office of Management and Budget
SCC	service center campus
TAC	Taxpayer Assistance Center

United States Government Accountability Office
Washington, DC 20548

June 28, 2012

The Honorable Douglas H. Shulman
Commissioner of Internal Revenue

Dear Mr. Shulman:

In its role as the nation's tax collector, the Internal Revenue Service (IRS) has a demanding responsibility to collect taxes, process tax returns, and enforce the nation's tax laws. In fiscal year 2011, IRS collected about $2.4 trillion in tax payments, processed hundreds of millions of federal tax and information returns, and paid about $416 billion in refunds to taxpayers. Because of its role and overall mission, IRS's activities affect virtually all of the nation's citizens. It is therefore critical that the agency strive to maintain sound internal control and financial management practices.

IRS has made significant progress in improving its internal controls and financial management since it was first required to prepare a set of financial statements nearly two decades ago. This progress is reflected in IRS's 12-year record of clean audit opinions on its financial statements and its resolution of several material weaknesses[1] and significant deficiencies[2] in internal controls over the years. At the same time, IRS continues to face significant financial management challenges in achieving the overarching goals of effective federal financial management—accountability and useful management information. To achieve its goals of effective financial and operational management, IRS

---

[1] A material weakness is a deficiency, or a combination of deficiencies, in internal control such that there is a reasonable possibility that a material misstatement of the entity's financial statements will not be prevented, or detected and corrected on a timely basis. A deficiency in internal control exists when the design or operation of a control does not allow management or employees, in the normal course of performing their assigned functions, to prevent, or detect and correct misstatements on a timely basis. Materiality represents the magnitude of an omission or misstatement of an item in a financial report that, when considered in light of surrounding circumstances, makes it probable that the judgment of a reasonable person relying on the information would have been changed or influenced by the inclusion or correction of the item.

[2] A significant deficiency is a deficiency, or a combination of deficiencies, in internal control that is less severe than a material weakness, yet important enough to merit attention by those charged with governance.

needs to (1) address its remaining material weaknesses and its significant deficiency in internal control, (2) fully integrate cost- and revenue-based outcome-oriented decision making into its tax collection enforcement operations, and (3) implement corrective actions to address other identified control deficiencies.

An agency's internal control serves as the first line of defense in safeguarding its assets and in preventing and detecting errors and fraud, as well as in helping to effectively manage its stewardship over public resources.[3] For many years, IRS has had control deficiencies in internal controls over fundamental elements of its operations that leave it vulnerable to a greater risk of fraud, waste, abuse, and mismanagement. During our audit of IRS's fiscal year 2011 financial statements,[4] we found that IRS continued to be challenged with two long-standing material weaknesses in internal control that are at the heart of its operations—weaknesses in internal controls over unpaid tax assessments (unpaid assessments)[5] and over information systems security. We also found that IRS continued to have a significant deficiency in internal control over the processing of manually prepared tax refunds and claims for the First-time Homebuyer Credit (FTHBC) that led to erroneous refund disbursements. In addition, as in past years, IRS management faces a challenge in enhancing and using its financial management capabilities to develop and

---

[3]Management is responsible for establishing and maintaining internal control to achieve the objectives of effective and efficient operations, reliable financial reporting, and compliance with applicable laws and regulations. See 31 U.S.C. § 3512(c), (d), commonly known as the Federal Managers' Financial Integrity Act of 1982 (FMFIA); see also, GAO, *Standards for Internal Control in the Federal Government*, GAO/AIMD-00-21.3.1 (Washington, D.C.: November 1999), 4-5. The actions required by agencies and individual federal managers includes taking proactive measures to develop and implement appropriate, cost-effective internal control for results-oriented management; to assess the adequacy of internal control in federal programs and operations; to identify needed improvements; and to take corresponding corrective actions.

[4]GAO, *Financial Audit: IRS's Fiscal Years 2011 and 2010 Financial Statements*, GAO-12-165 (Washington, D.C.: Nov. 10, 2011).

[5]An unpaid assessment is a legally enforceable claim against a taxpayer and consists of taxes, penalties, and interest that have not been collected or abated (a reduction in a tax assessment).

use outcome-oriented performance metrics[6] critical to providing the foundation upon which it can manage its operations for outcomes.

To assist IRS in strengthening its internal controls and improving its operations, over the years we have made numerous recommendations as part of our annual financial statement audits and other financial management–related work at IRS. This report (1) provides an overview of the continuing financial management challenges facing IRS; (2) describes the status of financial audit–related recommendations and the actions needed to address them, and (3) discusses how the unresolved recommendations are integrally related to control activities central to IRS's mission and goals.

Appendix I provides a summary of the status of GAO recommendations. To assist IRS in addressing those control activities, appendix II provides summary information regarding the primary control deficiencies to which each open recommendation is related. Our recommendations related to IRS's information systems security are reported separately because of the sensitive nature of many of the control deficiencies that give rise to the recommendations.[7] However, we do provide summary data on the number of information security–related recommendations and their general makeup. We are not making any new recommendations in this report.

Background

Internal control is not one event, but rather a series of activities that should occur throughout an entity's operations and on an ongoing basis. Internal control should be an integral part of each system that management uses to regulate and guide its operations, rather than as a separate system within an agency. In this sense, internal control is management control that should be built into the entity as a part of its

---

[6]The term "outcome-oriented performance metrics," refers to the measurement of the end result of a work activity or series of activities, such as the taxes collected as a result of a tax assessment and the collection actions taken by IRS employees, such as telephone calls to tax debtors.

[7]Although most of our recommendations regarding our information security work are sensitive and reported to IRS separately, we have reported our objectives, summary results, and nonsensitive recommendations in a publicly available report. See GAO, *Information Security: IRS Needs to Enhance Internal Control over Financial Reporting and Taxpayer Data*, GAO-12-393 (Washington, D.C.: Mar. 16, 2012).

infrastructure to help managers run the entity and achieve their goals on an ongoing basis.

Section 3512 (c), (d) of Title 31, U.S. Code, commonly known as the Federal Managers' Financial Integrity Act of 1982 (FMFIA), requires agencies to establish and maintain effective internal control. The agency head must annually evaluate and report on the control and financial systems that protect the integrity of its federal programs. The requirements of FMFIA serve as an umbrella under which other reviews, evaluations, and audits should be coordinated and considered to support management's assertion about the effectiveness of internal control over operations, financial reporting, and compliance with laws and regulations.

Office of Management and Budget (OMB) Circular No. A-123, Management's Responsibility for Internal Control, provides the implementing guidance for FMFIA, and prescribes the specific requirements for assessing and reporting on internal controls consistent with the Standards for Internal Control in the Federal Government (internal control standards) issued by the Comptroller General of the United States.[8] The circular defines management's responsibilities related to internal control and the required process for assessing internal control effectiveness, and provides specific requirements for conducting management's assessment of the effectiveness of internal control over financial reporting. The circular requires management to annually provide assurances on internal control and emphasizes the need for integrated and coordinated internal control assessments that synchronize all internal control–related activities.[9]

FMFIA requires GAO to issue standards for internal control in the federal government. The internal control standards provide the overall framework for establishing and maintaining effective internal control and for

---

[8]GAO/AIMD-00-21.3.1 (Washington, D.C.: Nov. 1, 1999) contains the internal control standards to be followed by executive agencies in establishing and maintaining systems of internal control as required by FMFIA.

[9]The circular requires agencies and individual federal managers to take systematic and proactive measures to (1) develop and implement appropriate, cost-effective internal control for results-oriented management; (2) assess the adequacy of internal control in federal programs and operations; (3) separately assess and document internal control over financial reporting consistent with the process defined in appendix A of the circular; (4) identify needed improvements; (5) take corresponding corrective action; and (6) report annually on internal control through management assurance statements.

identifying and addressing major performance and management challenges and areas at greatest risk of fraud, waste, abuse, and mismanagement.

As summarized in the internal control standards, internal control in the government is defined by the following five elements, which also provide the basis against which internal controls are to be evaluated:

- *Control environment*: Management and employees should establish and maintain an environment throughout the organization that sets a positive and supportive attitude toward internal control and conscientious management.

- *Risk assessment*: Internal control should provide for an assessment of the risks the agency faces from both external and internal sources.

- *Control activities*: Internal control activities help ensure that management's directives are carried out. The control activities should be effective and efficient in accomplishing the agency's control objectives.

- *Information and communication*: Information should be recorded and communicated to management and others within the entity who need it and in a form and within a time frame that enables them to carry out their internal control and other responsibilities.

- *Monitoring*: Internal control monitoring should assess the quality of performance over time and ensure that the findings of audits and other reviews are promptly resolved.

A key objective in our annual audits of IRS's financial statements is to obtain reasonable assurance that IRS maintained effective internal control with respect to financial reporting. While we use all five elements of internal control, including risk assessment and monitoring, as a basis for evaluating the effectiveness of IRS's internal controls, our ongoing evaluations and tests have focused heavily on control activities, where we have identified numerous control deficiencies and have provided recommendations for corrective action. Control activities are the policies, procedures, techniques, and mechanisms that are intended to enforce management's directives. In other words, they are the activities conducted in the everyday course of business that are intended to accomplish a control objective, such as ensuring IRS employees successfully complete background checks prior to being granted access to taxpayer information and receipts. Control activities are an integral part of an entity's planning, implementing, reviewing, and accountability for stewardship of government resources and achievement of effective results.

Scope and Methodology

To accomplish our objectives, we evaluated the effectiveness of corrective actions IRS implemented during fiscal year 2011 in response to open recommendations as part of our fiscal years 2011 and 2010 financial audits. To determine the status of the recommendations, we (1) obtained IRS's reported status of each recommendation and corrective action taken or planned as of March 2012, (2) compared IRS's reported status to our fiscal year 2011 audit findings to identify any differences between IRS's and our conclusions regarding the status of each recommendation, and (3) performed additional follow-up work to assess IRS's actions taken to address the open recommendations. Because of the sensitive nature of many of the issues related to our recommendations regarding information security, we have reported our recommendations for corrective action related to information security issues to IRS separately.[10]

In order to determine how IRS's open recommendations, including those identified in our June 2012 management report,[11] fit within the agency's management and internal control structure, we compared the open recommendations and the issues that gave rise to them to the (1) control activities listed in the internal control standards, (2) list of major factors and examples outlined in our Internal Control Management and Evaluation Tool,[12] and (3) criteria and objectives for federal financial management as discussed in the Chief Financial Officers Act of 1990 (CFO Act) and the Federal Accounting Standards Advisory Board's (FASAB) Statement of Federal Financial Accounting Concepts No. 1, Objectives of Federal Financial Reporting.[13] We also considered whether

---

[10]See GAO-12-393.

[11]GAO, *Management Report: Improvements Are Needed to Enhance the Internal Revenue Service's Internal Controls and Operating Effectiveness*, GAO-12-683R (Washington, D.C.: June 25, 2012).

[12]GAO, *Internal Control Standards: Internal Control Management and Evaluation Tool*, GAO-01-1008G (Washington, D.C.: Aug. 1, 2001).

[13]FASAB, Statement of Federal Financial Concepts No. 1: *Objectives of Federal Financial Reporting*, FASAB Handbook, Version 10 (Washington, D.C.: June 30, 2011).

IRS had addressed, in whole or in part, the underlying control deficiencies that gave rise to the recommendations; and other legal requirements and implementing guidance, such as FMFIA and OMB Circular No. A-123.

Our work was performed from December 2011 through April 2012 in accordance with generally accepted government auditing standards.

IRS Faces Continuing Significant Financial Management Challenges

IRS continues to make progress in resolving its control deficiencies and addressing outstanding recommendations, but continues to face significant financial management challenges. Since we first began auditing IRS's financial statements in fiscal year 1992, IRS has taken a significant number of actions that were sufficient to resolve several material weaknesses and significant control deficiencies and to close over 300 of our previously reported recommendations. This includes 38 recommendations we are closing with this report based on actions IRS took through March 2012.

Nevertheless, IRS continues to face challenges in establishing effective controls over its financial and operational management. Specifically, IRS continues to face management challenges in (1) resolving its two material weaknesses and one significant deficiency in internal control and (2) developing performance measures necessary to managing operational performance outcomes. Further, as in previous years' audits, our fiscal year 2011 audit continued to identify additional internal control deficiencies, resulting in 30 new recommendations for corrective action. These deficiencies and related recommendations are discussed in detail in our June 2012 management report to IRS.[14] In addition, as noted earlier, we also identified control deficiencies related to information security during our fiscal year 2011 audit that we reported separately with limited distribution because of the sensitive nature of many of those control deficiencies.[15]

[14]GAC-12-683R.

[15]See GAO-12-393.

Challenges in Resolving Two Long-standing Material Weaknesses and One Significant Deficiency in Internal Control

As in past years, IRS continued to face significant challenges in resolving its remaining long-standing material weaknesses in internal control concerning (1) unpaid assessments[16] and (2) information security in fiscal year 2011.

IRS's continuing challenge in addressing its material weakness in internal control over unpaid assessments results from its (1) inability to rely on its general ledger and underlying subsidiary records to report federal taxes receivable, compliance assessments, and writeoffs in accordance with federal accounting standards without significant compensating procedures; (2) inability to trace reported taxes receivable to supporting transactions and maintain an effective transaction-based subledger for unpaid assessment transactions; and (3) inability to effectively prevent or timely detect and correct errors in taxpayer accounts. These control deficiencies are caused primarily by IRS's continued reliance on software applications that were not designed to provide accurate, complete, and timely transaction-level financial information, as well as errors in taxpayer accounts. Consequently, IRS management is impaired in its ability to make well-informed decisions and to accumulate and report financial information in accordance with federal accounting standards. These problems are likely to continue to exist until these software applications are either significantly enhanced or replaced, and IRS remedies the control deficiencies that continue to result in significant errors in taxpayer accounts.

IRS's continuing challenge in addressing its material weakness in internal control over information systems security is primarily due to both continuing and newly identified control deficiencies. As in past years, IRS continued to (1) rely on a procurement system that lacks reliable controls due to access control deficiencies and database maintenance that was not performed; (2) use unencrypted protocols for a sensitive tax processing application; and (3) have unresolved physical security control

---

[16]Unpaid assessments are unpaid taxes. For reporting purposes, federal accounting standards classify unpaid assessments, including assessed penalties and accrued interest, into federal taxes receivables, compliance assessments, and writeoffs. Federal taxes receivable are taxes due from taxpayers for which IRS can support the existence of a receivable through taxpayer agreement or a favorable court ruling. Compliance assessments are assessments where neither the taxpayer nor the court has affirmed that the amounts are owed. Writeoffs represent unpaid tax assessments for which IRS does not expect further collection because of factors such as the taxpayer's death, bankruptcy, or insolvency.

deficiencies. Further, in fiscal year 2011, we identified control deficiencies in IRS's (1) system access and configuration controls and (2) controls intended to compensate and mitigate for known information security deficiencies. As a result of these control deficiencies considered collectively, IRS was (1) unable to rely upon its systems or compensating and mitigating controls to provide reasonable assurance that its financial statements were fairly presented, (2) unable to ensure the reliability of other financial management information produced by its systems, and (3) at increased risk of compromising confidential IRS and taxpayer information.

In addition to the continuing challenges posed by the two long-standing material weaknesses concerning unpaid assessments and information security, our audit of IRS's fiscal year 2011 financial statements[17] also identified a continuing significant deficiency in IRS's internal control over tax refund disbursements, specifically, controls over the processing of claims for the First-time Homebuyer Credit (FTHBC)[18] and over manual refunds. These control deficiencies related to the documentation of FTHBC claims, monitoring of manual refunds, and training of staff having key roles in refund processing.

Challenges in Developing and Implementing Performance Metrics to Assist in Managing for Outcomes

As in past years, IRS continues to face challenges in developing and institutionalizing the use of financial management information to assist it in making operational decisions and in measuring the effectiveness of its programs. IRS made progress during fiscal year 2011 in developing and integrating cost-based performance information into its operational decision-making processes. However, IRS has not yet fully integrated outcome-oriented cost-based performance data[19] into each business units' routine decision-making processes. IRS has also not yet integrated outcome-oriented performance data into its externally-reported performance metrics.

---

[17]GAO-12-165

[18]The FTHBC is codified, as amended, at 26 U.S.C. § 36. For an explanation of the FTHBC, see GAO-12-165, p. 9, footnote 9.

[19]An "outcome" is a measure of the end result of a work activity or series of activities, such as the taxes collected, and is a measure of the results of providing outputs.

During fiscal year 2011, IRS continued to add to the number of programs and activities for which full cost, and applicable return on investment (ROI), information has been developed. Further, for the past several years, IRS has annually updated the data for each set of such information. Additionally during fiscal year 2011, management teams in several of IRS's business units began to implement the use of available full cost information for decision making.

However, this progress in the use of programmatic full cost and ROI information, and related performance metrics, had not yet extended to IRS's primary business unit responsible for developing and directing IRS's corporate-wide enforcement activities to collect unpaid taxes. The integration of such information into both IRS's strategic and routine enforcement-related management decisions could greatly enhance IRS's ability to manage for outcomes by evaluating the efficiency and cost-effectiveness of its programs and activities, including comparing the efficiency and effectiveness of various existing enforcement collection strategies, staffing levels, and proposed changes.

Developing informative and reliable outcome-oriented performance metrics based on specific enforcement programs' costs and revenues would assist IRS in improving its ability to (1) establish measurable outcome goals, (2) evaluate the relative merits of various program options, and (3) highlight opportunities for optimizing the allocation of resources. They could also assist IRS in more credibly demonstrating to Congress and the public that it is using its appropriations cost-effectively.

A lack of outcome-oriented performance metrics is inconsistent with federal financial management concepts as embodied in the Federal Accounting Standards Advisory Board's (FASAB) Statement of Federal Financial Accounting Concepts No. 1, Objectives of Federal Financial Reporting.[20] Specifically, in its discussion of financial reporting concepts, FASAB notes that federal financial data should provide accountability and decision-useful information on the costs of programs and the outputs and outcomes achieved, and it should provide data for evaluating service efforts, costs, and accomplishments.

---

[20]FASAB, Statement of Federal Financial Concepts No. 1: *Objectives of Federal Financial Reporting*.

The absence of outcome metrics is also inconsistent with the objectives of the CFO Act. A key objective of the act was for agencies to routinely develop and use appropriate financial management information to evaluate program effectiveness, make fully informed operational decisions, and ensure accountability. While obtaining a clean audit opinion on its financial statements is important in itself, it is not the CFO Act's end goal. Rather, the act's end goal is modern financial management systems that provide reliable, timely, and useful financial information to support day-to-day decision making and oversight. Such systems and practices should also provide for the systematic measurement of both program outputs and outcomes.

We have made several recommendations to IRS over the years to address its financial management challenges in developing internal full cost data for its programs and activities and for outcome-oriented performance measures. Successfully addressing the remaining open recommendations would enhance IRS's ability to effectively manage for outcomes.

Status of Recommendations Based on the Fiscal Year 2011 Financial Statement Audit

In June 2011, we reported on the status of IRS's efforts to implement corrective actions to address recommendations stemming from our fiscal year 2010 and prior years' financial statement audits and other financial management–related work.[21] In that report, we identified 77 audit recommendations that remained open and thus required corrective action by IRS. A significant number of these recommendations had been open for several years, either because IRS had not taken corrective action or because the actions taken had not yet effectively resolved the control deficiencies that gave rise to the recommendations.

IRS has continued to work to address many of the control deficiencies related to these previously reported open recommendations. In the course of performing our fiscal year 2011 financial audit, we determined IRS took actions sufficient to address 38 of our prior years' recommendations. However, a total of 39 recommendations from prior years remain open, a significant number of which have been outstanding for several years. IRS considers 16 of the prior years' recommendations

---

[21] GAO, *Internal Revenue Service: Status of GAO Financial Audit and Related Financial Management Report Recommendations*, GAO-11-536 (Washington, D.C.: June 22, 2011).

to be effectively addressed and therefore closed. However, we consider them to remain open. For 14 of the 16, in our view, IRS's actions did not fully address the control deficiencies that gave rise to the recommendations. For the remaining two, we have not yet been able to verify the effectiveness of IRS's actions. The "Status per IRS" and "Status per GAO" sections of appendix I provide a summary of both IRS's and our assessment of IRS's actions on each recommendation.

During our audit of IRS's fiscal year 2011 financial statements, we identified additional control deficiencies that require corrective action. In our June 2012 management report to IRS,[22] we discussed these control deficiencies, and made 30 new recommendations to address them. Consequently, a total of 69 financial management–related recommendations need to be addressed—39 from prior years and 30 new recommendations resulting from our fiscal year 2011 audit. We consider all of the new recommendations to be correctible in the short term.[23] We also consider the majority of the recommendations outstanding from prior years to be correctible in the short term. However, a few, particularly those concerning the functionality of IRS's automated systems, are complex and may reasonably require several more years to fully and effectively address.

In addition to the 69 open recommendations from our financial audits, there are 118 additional open recommendations stemming from our assessment of IRS's information security controls over key financial systems, information, and interconnected networks conducted as an integral part of our annual financial audits. The control deficiencies that led to our previously reported and our newly identified recommendations related to information security increase the risk of unauthorized disclosure, modification, or destruction of financial and sensitive taxpayer data. Collectively, they constitute material weakness in IRS's internal control over information security for its financial and tax processing systems. As discussed previously, we are reporting our recommendations resulting from the information security control deficiencies identified in our

---

[22]GAO-12-683R.

[23]We define short term recommendations as those that we believe could be addressed within 2 years from the time we made the recommendation. We define long term recommendations as those we expect to require 2 years or more to implement from the time we made the recommendation.

annual audits of IRS's financial statements separately because of the sensitive nature of many of these control deficiencies.[24]

Appendix I presents a summary of the status of IRS actions to address 107 GAO non-information security-related recommendations based on our financial audits—77 from our audits prior to fiscal year 2011 and 30 new recommendations based on the results of our fiscal year 2011 financial audit. Appendix I consists of the (1) recommendation, (2) GAO report in which the recommendation was made, (3) IRS-reported status of corrective actions taken or planned as of March 2012, and (3) our analysis of the status of IRS actions as to whether those actions effectively addressed the deficiencies that gave rise to the recommendation. Appendix I lists the recommendations by the year in which the recommendation was made and by GAO report number.

Appendix II presents the 69 open recommendations that remained at the end of our fiscal year 2011 audit as a result of closing the aforementioned 38 recommendations and adding 30 new recommendations, grouped by related material weakness, significant deficiency, and compliance issue as described in our audit report on IRS's financial statements,[25] as well as other control deficiencies we have identified and discussed in our annual management reports to IRS.[26]

Open Recommendations Grouped by Internal Control Activity

Linking the open recommendations from our financial audits, and the control deficiencies that gave rise to them, to internal control activities that are central to IRS's tax administration responsibilities provides insight regarding their significance to accomplishing IRS's mission.

As discussed earlier, internal control standards define internal control as consisting of five elements—control environment, risk assessment, control activities, information and communication, and monitoring.[27] For the control activities element, the internal control standards explain that an agency's system of internal control should provide for an assessment

---

[24]See GAO-12-393.

[25]GAO-12-165.

[26]See GAO-12-683R for the recommendations resulting from our fiscal year 2011 audit.

[27]GAO/AIMD-00-21.3.1.

of the risks the agency faces from both external and internal sources and that internal control activities should help ensure that management's directives and related control objectives are carried out. The control activities element identified 11 specific control activities, which we have grouped into three categories, as shown in table 1. Each of the unresolved recommendations from our financial audits, and the underlying control deficiencies that gave rise to them, can be grouped into one of the 11 specific control activities as shown in table 1.

Table 1: Summary of Recommendations Grouped by Control Activity

Control activity	Open at the beginning of 2011	Closed during 2011 audit	New from 2011 audit	Total remaining open	Percentage
Safeguarding of assets and security activities					
Physical control over vulnerable assets	22	9	0	13	19
Segregation of duties	1	1	1	1	1
Controls over information processing	0	0	0	0	0
Access restrictions to and accountability for resources and records	6	2	0	4	6
Subtotal	**29**	**12**	**1**	**18**	**26**
Proper recording and documenting of transactions					
Appropriate documentation of transactions and internal controls	13	10	5	8	12
Accurate and timely recording of transactions and events	15	6	7	16	23
Proper execution of transactions and events	2	2	5	5	7
Subtotal	**30**	**18**	**17**	**29**	**42**
Effective management review and oversight					
Reviews by management at the functional or activity level	13	5	10	18	27
Establishment and review of performance measures and indicators	1	0	0	1	1
Management of human capital	4	3	2	3	4
Top-level reviews of actual performance	0	0	0	0	0
Subtotal	**18**	**8**	**12**	**22**	**32**
Total	**77**	**38**	**30**	**69**	**100**

Source: GAO.

As shown in table 1, 18 (26 percent) of the unresolved recommendations relate to IRS's controls over safeguarding of assets and security activities, 29 (42 percent) relate to control deficiencies associated with IRS's ability to properly record and document transactions, and 22 (32 percent) relate to control deficiencies associated with IRS's management review and oversight.

In the following section, we group the 69 open recommendations under the specific control activity to which the condition that gave rise to each recommendation most appropriately fits. We define each control activity as presented in the internal control standards and briefly identify some of the key IRS operations that fall under that control activity. Although not comprehensive, the descriptions are intended to help explain why actions to strengthen these control activities are important for IRS to efficiently and effectively carry out its overall mission.

Each control activity description includes a table of the related open recommendations. The tables list the recommendations by the year in which we made them (ID no.). At the end of our description of each recommendation, we also provide an assessment of whether the recommendation can be addressed in the short term or long term. We judged a recommendation to be correctible in the short term when we believe that IRS had the capability to implement solutions within 2 years of the year in which we first reported the control deficiency and made the recommendations.

Safeguarding of Assets and Security Activities

Given IRS's mission, the sensitivity of the data it maintains, and its responsibility for processing trillions of dollars of tax receipts each year, one of the most important control activities at IRS is safeguarding assets. Internal control in this important area should be designed to provide reasonable assurance regarding prevention or prompt detection of unauthorized acquisition, use, or disposition of an agency's assets. IRS has outstanding recommendations in the following three control activities related to safeguarding and securing assets: (1) physical control over vulnerable assets, (2) segregation of duties, and (3) access restrictions to, and accountability for, resources and records.

Physical Control over Vulnerable Assets

> *Internal control standard:* An agency must establish physical control to secure and safeguard vulnerable assets. Examples include security for and limited access to assets such as cash, securities, inventories, and equipment which might be vulnerable to risk of loss or unauthorized use. Such assets should be periodically counted and compared to control records.

Of the trillions of dollars in taxes that IRS collects each year, hundreds of billions is collected in the form of checks and cash accompanied by tax returns and related information.[28] IRS collects taxes both at its own facilities as well as at lockbox banks.[29] IRS acts as custodian for (1) tax payments it receives until they are deposited in the General Fund of the U.S. Treasury and (2) tax returns and related information it receives until they are either sent to the Federal Records Center or destroyed. IRS is also charged with controlling many other assets, such as computers and other equipment. IRS's legal responsibility to safeguard tax returns and the confidential information taxpayers provide on those returns makes the effectiveness of IRS's internal controls over physical security essential to accomplishing its mission.

While effective physical safeguards over receipts should exist throughout the year, such safeguards are especially important during the peak tax filing season. Each year during the weeks preceding and shortly after April 15, an IRS service center[30] or lockbox bank may receive and process daily over 100,000 pieces of mail containing returns, receipts, or both. The dollar value of receipts each service center and lockbox bank processes increases to hundreds of millions of dollars a day during this time frame.

The following 13 open recommendations in table 2 are designed to improve IRS's physical controls over vulnerable assets. They include

---

[28]The majority of federal tax payments are made for both businesses and individuals through the Electronic Federal Tax Payment System.

[29]Lockbox banks operate under contract with the Department of the Treasury's (Treasury) Financial Management Service. The three lockbox banks perform processing functions in seven locations throughout the United States.

[30]Five of IRS's 10 service center campuses (SCC) process tax returns and payments submitted by taxpayers.

recommendations for IRS to improve controls over physical security at its Taxpayer Assistance Centers (TAC)[31] and courier activities. We consider all of these recommendations to be correctable in the short term.

Table 2: Open Recommendations to Improve IRS's Physical Controls over Vulnerable Assets

ID no.	Recommendation
06-05	Equip all Taxpayer Assistance Centers (TAC) with adequate physical security controls to deter and prevent unauthorized access to restricted areas or office space occupied by other IRS units, including those TACs that are not scheduled to be reconfigured to the "new TAC" model in the near future. This includes appropriately separating customer service waiting areas from restricted areas in the near future by physical barriers, such as locked doors marked with signs barring entrance by unescorted customers. (short-term)
07-04	Develop and implement appropriate corrective actions for any gaps in closed circuit television (CCTV) camera coverage that do not provide an unobstructed view of the entire exterior of the service center campus's (SCC) perimeter, such as adding or repositioning existing CCTV cameras or removing obstructions. (short-term)
09-03	Document in the Internal Revenue Manual (IRM) minimum requirements for establishing criteria for time discrepancies or other inconsistencies, which if noted as part of the required monitoring of Form 10160, Receipt for Transport of IRS Deposit, would require off-site surveillance of couriers. (short-term)
09-06	Establish procedures to ensure that an inventory of all duress alarms is documented for each location and is readily available to individuals conducting duress alarm tests before each test is conducted. (short-term)
09-07	Establish procedures to periodically update the inventory of duress alarms at each Taxpayer Assistance Center (TAC) location to ensure that the inventory is current and complete as of the testing date. (short-term)
09-08	Provide instructions for conducting quarterly duress alarm tests to ensure that IRS officials conducting the test (1) document the test results for each duress alarm listed in the inventory, including date, findings, and planned corrective action and (2) track the findings until they are properly resolved. (short-term)
09-09	Establish procedures requiring that each physical security analyst conduct a periodic documented review of the Emergency Signal History Report and emergency contact list for its respective location to ensure that (1) appropriate corrective actions have been planned for all incidents reported by the central monitoring station and (2) the emergency contact list for each location is current and includes only appropriate contacts. (short-term)
10-19	Establish procedures to track service center campus (SCC) acknowledgments of unprocessable items with receipts. (short-term)
10-20	Establish procedures to monitor the process used by service center campuses (SCC) and lockbox banks to acknowledge and track transmittals of unprocessable items with receipts. These procedures should include monitoring discrepancies and instituting appropriate corrective actions as needed. (short-term)
11-14	Establish procedures to provide a consistent methodology for calculating and establishing allowable deposit courier trip time limits to be used by both service center campuses (SCC) and lockbox banks that would assist in detecting potential unauthorized stops or other contractual violations by deposit couriers. Such procedures should include instructions for documenting and supporting how the trip limits were determined and require justification and approval for all established time limits that exceed the average trip time. (short-term)
11-16	Enforce existing contractual requirements for the cargo doors of contract courier vehicles to be locked after picking up taxpayer information. (short-term)

[31]IRS's 398 TACs are small field assistance units located in various cities and towns in every state, are part of IRS's Wage and Investment (W&I) operating division, and are designated to serve taxpayers who choose to seek help from IRS in person.

ID no.	Recommendation
11-17	Establish procedures to prevent or detect unauthorized access to taxpayer information in contract courier vehicles during transit. These procedures should detail specific activities to be performed by both the business unit sending and receiving the information transported by the contract courier. (short-term)
11-18	Revise the guidance for conducting the periodic reviews of the contract couriers transporting taxpayer information from one IRS processing facility to another to include procedures for (1) physically verifying that courier vehicle cargo doors are locked after picking up this information and remain locked during transit to the final destination and (2) documenting the basis for the reviewer's conclusions. (short-term)

Source: GAO.

Segregation of Duties

> *Internal control standard:* Key duties and responsibilities need to be divided or segregated among different people to reduce the risk of error or fraud. This should include separating the responsibilities for authorizing transactions, processing and recording them, reviewing the transactions, and handling any related assets. No one individual should control all key aspects of a transaction or event.

As discussed previously, IRS employees process hundreds of billions of dollars in tax receipts in the form of cash and checks. Consequently, it is critical that IRS maintain appropriate separation of duties so that no single individual would be in a position of causing an error or irregularity, or potentially converting the asset to personal use, and then concealing it. For example, when an IRS field office receives taxpayer receipts and returns, it is responsible for depositing the cash and checks in a depository institution and forwarding the related taxpayer information received for further processing, including updating the taxpayer's tax account records. In order to adequately safeguard receipts from theft, the person responsible for recording the information from the taxpayer receipts on a voucher should not also update the taxpayer's tax records.

Implementing the following recommendation in table 3 would help IRS improve its separation of duties, which will in turn strengthen controls over tax receipts. This recommendation is correctible in the short-term.

Table 3: Open Recommendation to Improve IRS's Segregation of Duties

ID no.	Recommendation
12-10	Update the Internal Revenue Manual (IRM) to specify steps to be followed to prevent campus support clerks as well as any other employees who process payments through the electronic check presentment system from making adjustments to taxpayer accounts. (short-term)

Source: GAO.

Access Restrictions to and Accountability for Resources and Records

> *Internal control standard:* Access to resources and records should be limited to authorized individuals, and accountability for their custody and use should be assigned and maintained. Periodic comparison of resources with the recorded accountability should be made to help reduce the risk of errors, fraud, misuse, or unauthorized alteration.

Because IRS is responsible for maintaining accountability over a large volume of cash and checks, it is imperative that it maintain strong controls to appropriately restrict access to those assets, the records relied on to track those assets, and sensitive taxpayer information. Our financial audits over the years have identified control deficiencies related to (1) individuals having direct access to cash and checks receiving appropriate background investigations before being granted access to taxpayer receipts and information and (2) maintaining effective access security control. The following four short term recommendations in table 4 are intended to help IRS improve its access restrictions to assets and records.

Table 4: Open Recommendations to Improve IRS's Access Restrictions to and Accountability for Resources and Records

ID no.	Recommendation
10-29	Analyze the various contractor access arrangements and establish a policy that requires security awareness training for all IRS contractors who are provided unescorted physical access to its facilities or taxpayer receipts and information. (short-term)
11-11	Perform a review of all existing contracts under $100,000 that (1) do not have an appointed contracting officer's technical representative (COTR) and (2) do not require that contract employees obtain background investigations to assess whether the services performed under each contract warrant a requirement that contract employees obtain background investigations. (short-term)
11-12	Based on a review of all existing contracts under $100,000 without an appointed COTR that should require contract employees to obtain favorable background investigation results, amend those contracts to require that favorable background investigations be obtained for all relevant contract employees before routine, unescorted, unsupervised physical access to taxpayer information is granted. (short-term)
11-13	Establish a policy requiring collaborative oversight between IRS's key offices in determining whether potential service contracts involve routine, unescorted, unsupervised physical access to taxpayer information, thus requiring background investigations, regardless of contract award amount. This policy should include a process for the requiring business unit to communicate to the Office of Procurement and the Human Capital Office the services to be provided under the contract and any potential exposure of taxpayer information to contract employees providing the services, and for all three units to (1) evaluate the risk of exposure of taxpayer information prior to finalizing and awarding the contract and (2) ensure that the final contract requires favorable background investigations as applicable, commensurate with the assessed risk. (short-term)

Source: GAO.

Proper Recording and Documenting of Transactions

IRS has a number of control deficiencies related to recording transactions, documenting events, and tracking the processing of taxpayer receipts or information. IRS has outstanding recommendations in the following three control activities related to proper recording and documenting of transactions: (1) appropriate documentation of transactions and internal controls, (2) accurate and timely recording of transactions and events, and (3) proper execution of transactions and events.

Appropriate Documentation of Transactions and Internal Control

Internal control standard: Internal control and all transactions and other significant events need to be clearly documented, and the documentation should be readily available for examination. The documentation should appear in management directives, administrative policies, or operating manuals and may be in paper or electronic form. All documentation and records should be properly managed and maintained.

IRS collects and processes trillions of dollars in taxpayer receipts annually both at its own facilities and at lockbox banks under contract to process taxpayer receipts for the federal government. Therefore, it is important that IRS maintain effective controls to ensure that all documents and records are properly and timely recorded, managed, and maintained both at its facilities and at the lockbox banks. In this regard, it is critical that IRS adequately document and disseminate its procedures to ensure that they are available for IRS employees. IRS must also document its management reviews of controls, such as those regarding refunds and returned checks, document transmittals, and reviews of Taxpayers Assistance Center (TAC) operations. To ensure future availability of adequate documentation, IRS must ensure that (1) its systems, particularly those now being developed and implemented, have appropriate capability to identify and trace individual transactions and (2) all critical steps in its accounting processes are adequately documented. Resolving the following eight recommendations in table 5 would assist IRS in improving its documentation of transactions and related internal control procedures. All of these recommendations are correctible in the short term.

Table 5: Open Recommendations to Improve IRS's Documentation of Transactions and Internal Control

ID no.	Recommendation
05-39	Enforce requirements for documenting monitoring actions and supervisory review for manual refunds. (short-term)
06-02	Enforce compliance with existing requirements that all IRS units transmitting taxpayer receipts and information from one IRS facility to another, including service center campuses (SCC), Taxpayer Assistance Centers (TAC), and units within the Large Business and International (LB&I) and the Tax-Exempt and Government Entities (TE/GE) business operating units, establish a system to track acknowledged copies of document transmittals. (short-term)
11-24	Revise the post orders for the SCC and lockbox bank security guards to include specific procedures for timely reporting exterior lighting outages to SCC or lockbox bank facilities management. These procedures should specify (1) whom to contact to report lighting outages and (2) how to document and track lighting outages until resolved. (short-term)
12-05	Update IRS's procedures for comparing tax revenue recorded in the general ledger to detailed tax revenue transactions recorded in the master files to (1) establish minimum criteria defining a significant or unusual variance and (2) specify the steps required to effectively evaluate and resolve these variances. (short-term)
12-06	Update IRS's procedures for comparing tax revenue recorded in the general ledger to detailed tax revenue transactions recorded in the master files to require that management reviews ensure preparers evaluate and resolve unusual or significant variances. (short-term)
12-13	Revise existing written procedures to require supervisory review of the Computer-Aided Facilities Management (CAFM) Quarterly Review Certifications and Statistics against the Graphic Database Interface system (GDI) validation walkthrough sheets. (short-term)
12-14	Establish mechanisms to monitor the implementation of and compliance with the revised policy established in October 2011 that requires field CAFM program managers to maintain GDI Quarterly Review documentation, including GDI validation walkthrough sheets and GDI Quarterly Review certifications. (short-term)
12-15	Establish mechanisms to monitor the implementation of and compliance with the revised policy established in October 2011 that defines the type of errors that should be captured on the CAFM Quarterly Review Certifications to help ensure that field CAFM program managers consistently compile the errors found in their quarterly reviews for compilation in the overall CAFM Quarterly Review Statistics. (short-term)

Source: GAO.

Accurate and Timely Recording of Transactions and Events

> *Internal control standard:* Transactions should be promptly recorded to maintain their relevance and value to management in controlling operations and making decisions. This applies to the entire process or life cycle of a transaction or event from the initiation and authorization through its final classification in summary records. In addition, control activities help to ensure that all transactions are completely and accurately recorded.

IRS has stewardship responsibility for maintaining sensitive records of tens of millions of taxpayers in addition to its responsibility for maintaining its own financial records. To maintain these records, IRS often has to rely on outdated computer systems or manual work-arounds. Unfortunately, some of IRS's recordkeeping difficulties we have reported on over the years will not be fully addressed until it can replace its aging systems; an effort that is long term and, in part, dependent on obtaining future funding.

Implementation of the following 16 recommendations in table 6 would strengthen IRS's recordkeeping abilities. Fifteen of these recommendations are short term, and one is long term regarding requirements for new systems for maintaining taxpayer records. Several of the recommendations listed deal with financial reporting processes, such as maintaining subsidiary records, recording budgetary transactions, and tracking program costs. Some of the control deficiencies that gave rise to several of our recommendations directly affect taxpayers, such as those involving duplicate assessments and errors in calculating and reporting interest and penalties. One of these recommendations has remained open for over 10 years, reflecting the complex nature of the underlying systems control deficiencies that must be resolved to fully address some of these control deficiencies.

Table 6: Open Recommendations to Improve IRS's Accurate and Timely Recording of Transactions and Events

ID no.	Recommendation
99-01	Manually review and eliminate duplicate or other assessments that have already been paid off to assure that all accounts related to a single assessment are appropriately credited for payments received. (short-term)
08-06	In instances where computer programs that control penalty assessments are not functioning in accordance with the intent of the Internal Revenue Manual (IRM), take appropriate action to correct the programs so that they function in accordance with the IRM. (long-term)
10-01	Review the results of IRS's unpaid assessments compensating statistical estimation process to identify and document instances where systemic limitations in the Custodial Detail Data Base (CDDB) resulted in misclassifications of account balances that, in turn, resulted in material inaccuracies in the amounts of reported unpaid assessments. (short-term)
10-02	Research and implement programming changes to allow CDDB to more accurately classify such accounts among the three categories of unpaid tax assessments. (short-term)
10-03	Research and identify control weaknesses resulting in inaccuracies or errors in taxpayer accounts that materially affect the financial reporting of unpaid tax assessments. (short-term)
10-04	Once IRS identifies the control weaknesses that result in inaccuracies or errors that materially affect the financial reporting of unpaid tax assessments, implement control procedures to routinely prevent, or to detect and correct, such errors. (short-term)
11-04	Establish formal written procedures requiring staff to review purchase contract terms against the goods and services received to date before requesting additional goods or services. (short-term)
11-05	Establish procedures to centrally review and monitor the timeliness of personnel action requests and approvals to help ensure compliance with the IRM and applicable Office of Personnel Management (OPM) regulations and guidance. (short-term)
11-26	Take steps to effectively implement the procedures requiring property staff to verify that the asset purchase price shown in the Asset Management Report agrees with the asset purchase price shown in the Integrated Financial System (IFS) and to resolve any variances before entering the information into the Information Technology Asset Management System (ITAMS). (short-term)

ID no.	Recommendation
12-07	Establish and document procedures for ensuring that recorded reimbursable revenue, transfers in without reimbursement, and accounts receivable from the Department of the Treasury Forfeiture Fund (TFF) conform to federal accounting standards. (short-term)
12-16	Establish procedures to require the Office of Financial Reporting to ensure that extracted Graphic Database Interface system (GDI) data used to calculate the leasehold improvement disposal estimate is complete and accurate. (short-term)
12-20	Establish a mechanism to periodically monitor contracting officers and contracting officers' technical representatives (COTR) compliance with the requirement to obtain and document end user confirmation of receipt prior to entering receipt and acceptance into the procurement system. (short-term)
12-21	Establish a mechanism for monitoring compliance with the existing requirement for employees and timekeepers to charge labor time spent on the Patient Protection and Affordable Care Act (PPACA) projects to the PPACA accounting code, such as through issuing periodic alerts, providing training and guidance, and/or having managers perform periodic reviews of employee labor time charges. (short-term)
12-22	Design and implement procedures specifying the review steps required to identify and research all transactions identified with a PPACA internal order number in the agency's expense files to confirm that they are PPACA-related expenses and, if so, to ensure that they are charged to the PPACA appropriation where appropriate. (short-term)
12-26	Implement an edit control in IRS's time card system to identify and prevent the processing of timecards that have not been electronically signed. (short-term)
12-30	Establish and document procedures for payroll staff to research and correct recycled errors from payroll processing on a regular and timely basis. (short-term)

Source: GAO.

Proper Execution of Transactions and Events

> *Internal control standard:* Transactions and other significant events should be authorized and executed only by persons acting within the scope of their authority. This is the principal means of ensuring that only valid transactions to exchange, transfer, use, or commit resources and other events are initiated or entered into. Authorizations should be clearly communicated to managers and employees.

IRS has thousands of leases that must be managed and properly recorded in its property records. IRS also has thousands of employees whose time and attendance must be properly recorded and approved so that IRS can appropriately manage its payroll expenditures. The following five short term recommendations in table 7 would improve IRS's controls over those areas.

Table 7: Open Recommendations to Improve IRS's Proper Execution of Transactions and Events

ID no.	Recommendation
12-17	Implement the revised January 2012 procedures requiring comparison of the leases used in the prior year with the current year leases to help ensure that expired leases have not been extended and thus, are only counted once in the disposal estimates. (short-term)
12-18	Implement the revised January 2012 procedures requiring preparation and review of leasehold improvement disposal calculations quarterly. (short-term)

ID no.	Recommendation
12-23	Revise the payroll standard operating procedures to specify steps that the human resource specialists are required to follow to ensure that each electronic time card is signed by an authorized official before the timecard is transmitted to the National Finance Center for processing and payment. (short-term)
12-24	Revise the payroll standard operating procedures to require that the designated proxy for a manager required to approve time cards be at an equivalent or higher level as the manager, consistent with the Internal Revenue Manual (IRM). (short-term)
12-25	Incorporate in the planned 2012 policy change requiring the manager or designated proxy to sign the electronic time card before transmitting payroll records to the National Finance Center the requirement that the designated proxy be at an equivalent or higher level than the employee's manager. (short-term)

Source: GAO.

Effective Management Review and Oversight

All personnel within IRS have an important role in establishing and maintaining effective internal control, but IRS's managers have additional review and oversight responsibilities. Management must monitor and evaluate controls to ensure that they are followed. Without adequate monitoring by managers, there is a risk that internal control activities may not be carried out effectively and in a timely manner. IRS has outstanding recommendations in the following three control activities related to effective management review and oversight: (1) reviews by management at the functional or activity level, (2) establishment and review of performance measures and indicators, and (3) management of human capital.

Reviews by Management at the Functional or Activity Level

Internal control standard: Managers need to compare actual performance to planned or expected results throughout the organization and analyze significant differences.

IRS is responsible for managing a large, complex organization. It employs and must oversee the activities of over 100,000 full-time and seasonal employees, which includes managing related personnel actions. IRS is also responsible for overseeing lockbox banks that process tens of thousands of individual receipts totaling hundreds of billions of dollars, monitoring the work of hundreds of contractors and numerous off-site processing facilities, issuing tax refunds, managing tax liens, and preparing financial records.

Effective management oversight of such large, complex operations is imperative for IRS to effectively and efficiently accomplish its mission. Implementing the following 17 short term and 1 long term recommendations in table 8 would improve IRS's management oversight of its operations. One of these recommendations has remained open for over 10 years, reflecting the complexities of the deficiencies involved in ensuring that tax liens are released timely.

Table 8: Open Recommendations to Improve IRS's Reviews by Management at the Functional or Activity Level

ID no.	Recommendation
01-06	Implement procedures to closely monitor the release of tax liens to ensure that they are released within 30 days of the date the related tax liability is fully satisfied. As part of these procedures, IRS should carefully analyze the causes of the delays in releasing tax liens identified by our work and prior work by IRS's former internal audit function and ensure that such procedures effectively address these issues. (short-term)
05-33	Enforce the requirement that a document transmittal form listing the enclosed Daily Report of Collection Activity forms be included in transmittal packages, using such methods as more frequent inspections or increased reliance on error reports compiled by the service center teller units receiving the information. (short-term)
05-38	Enforce requirements for monitoring accounts and reviewing monitoring of accounts for manual refunds. (short-term)
08-14	Revise the Internal Revenue Manual (IRM) to include a requirement that IRS conduct periodic, unannounced inspections at off-site contractor facilities entrusted with sensitive IRS information; document the results, including identification of any security issues; and verify that the contractor has taken appropriate corrective actions on any security issues observed. (short-term)
09-05	Establish procedures to track and routinely report the total dollar amounts and volumes of receipts collected by individual Taxpayer Assistance Center (TAC) location, group, territory, area, and nationwide. (long-term)
11-01	Put procedures in place to periodically monitor the effectiveness of the new First-time Homebuyer Credit (FTHBC) validity checks for the duration of the filing of FTHBC claims to verify that they are working as intended. (short-term)
11-02	Establish a mechanism to enforce the existing requirement for appropriate managers to immediately notify the manual refund units of any personnel changes affecting the approval or processing of manual refunds. This may be accomplished through mechanisms such as issuing periodic alerts, providing training or having the manual refund unit perform quarterly validations of the list of manual refund approving officials, or a combination of these. (short-term)
11-25	Revise the nature and scope of the service center campuses' (SCC) and lockbox banks' physical security reviews to include periodic after dark assessments of physical security controls. (short-term)
12-01	Establish and document an inventory of the specific systems involved in IRS's financial reporting process, including (1) describing what role each system plays in the financial reporting process, (2) concluding whether each system is considered to be material to financial reporting and why, and (3) denoting whether each system is controlled by IRS or by an external service provider and, if the latter, identifying the service provider. (short-term)
12-02	Enhance existing policies and procedures pertaining to monitoring internal control over the automated systems operated by IRS personnel to specifically provide for routine, documented monitoring of the specific internal controls within its financial reporting systems that are intended to ensure the integrity of the data reported in the financial statements and other financial reports. This monitoring process should (1) involve both automated systems specialists and individuals with expertise in accounting and reporting, as appropriate, (2) encompass the specific automated internal controls that affect the authorizing, processing, transmitting, or reporting of material financial transactions, and (3) be designed to determine whether these internal controls are in place and operating effectively. (short-term)
12-03	For any system identified as material to IRS's financial reporting process which is controlled by an external service provider, establish policies and procedures requiring and defining a routine, documented process for coordinating with the service provider to appropriately monitor related internal control. This may entail establishing an agreement with each service provider to allow IRS personnel the access to either (1) the system concerned, as necessary to perform appropriate monitoring of internal control over financial reporting, or (2) periodic reports prepared in accordance with Statements on Standards for Attestation Engagements (SSAE) No. 16 documenting the results of monitoring performed by the service provider. (short-term)

ID no.	Recommendation
12-04	Establish policies and procedures with respect to any external financial reporting system IRS personnel themselves do not directly monitor that specify required steps to routinely review periodic reports prepared by service providers' auditors in accordance with SSAE No. 16, including steps to document (1) an assessment of whether a review's scope, methodology, and timing is appropriate to satisfy IRS's objectives; (2) any control deficiencies disclosed in the report, and an assessment of their materiality to IRS's financial reporting process and related risks; and (3) any compensating internal controls needed to mitigate any actual or potential effects of identified deficiencies upon IRS's internal and external financial reports resulting from any (a) material weakness, or (b) significant shortcoming in the scope, methodology, or timing of any SSAE No. 16 report reviewed relative to IRS's internal control objectives. (short-term)
12-08	Establish requirements specifying a required time frame for territory managers to perform the required review and approval of completed audit management checklists. (short-term)
12-09	Establish procedures requiring Physical Security and Emergency Preparedness (PSEP) headquarters to centrally monitor compliance with the audit management checklist process to ensure that (1) PSEP analysts timely complete their physical security reviews using the proper audit management checklists and (2) territory managers timely review and properly document their reviews of completed audit management checklists. (short-term)
12-11	Implement the September 2011 revised policy that requires an independent review of the rent check summary report to help ensure that the monthly rent allocation process is properly completed. (short-term)
12-12	Establish a policy requiring an independent review of changes made by the rent processing administrator to non-GSA lease data in the Graphic Database Interface system (GDI). (short-term)
12-28	Establish procedures for human resource specialists to track and monitor supervisory actions taken for employees with less than fully successful ratings that have a within-grade pay increase due date within 90 days to include specific required steps for following-up with managers to ensure the managers properly issue the employees a 60-day notification letter providing them an opportunity to improve their performance, make a timely determination on releasing or denying a within-grade pay increase, and properly carry out the requirements necessary to support the decision made. (short-term)
12-29	Establish procedures for HR specialists to track and monitor supervisory actions taken for employees with less than fully successful ratings that have a within-grade pay increase due date within 90 days to include specific required steps for timely granting a within-grade pay increase to such employees who were not given a 60-day notification letter. (short-term)

Source: GAO.

Establishment and Review of Performance Measures and Indicators

Internal control standard: Activities need to be established to monitor performance measures and indicators. These controls could call for comparisons and assessments relating different sets of data to one another so that analyses of the relationships can be made and appropriate actions taken. Controls should also be aimed at validating the propriety and integrity of both organizational and individual performance measures and indicators.

IRS's operations include a wide range of activities, including educating taxpayers, processing taxpayer receipts and data, disbursing hundreds of billions of dollars in refunds to millions of taxpayers, maintaining extensive information on tens of millions of taxpayers, and seeking collection from individuals and businesses that fail to comply with the nation's tax laws. Within its compliance function, IRS has numerous activities, including identifying businesses and individuals that underreport income, collecting from taxpayers who do not pay taxes, and collecting from those receiving refunds to which they are not entitled. Consequently, it is vitally important for IRS to have sound performance measures and related data to assist it in assessing its performance and targeting resources to maximize the return on investment.

The following long term recommendation in table 9 is designed to assist IRS in evaluating its operations and determining which activities are the most beneficial. This recommendation is directed at improving IRS's ability to measure and evaluate program performance costs, benefits, and operational outcomes—particularly with regard to identifying its most cost-effective tax collection activities.

Table 9: Open Recommendation to Improve IRS's Establishment and Review of Performance Measures and Indicators

ID no.	Recommendation
09-16	Develop outcome-oriented performance measures and related performance goals for IRS's enforcement programs and activities that include measures of the full cost of, and the revenue collected from, those programs and activities (return on investment) to assist IRS's managers in optimizing resource allocation decisions and evaluating the effectiveness of their activities. (long-term)

Source: GAO.

Management of Human Capital

Internal control standard: Effective management of an organization's workforce—its human capital—is essential to achieving results and an important part of internal control. Management should view human capital as an asset rather than a cost. Only when the right personnel for the job are on board and are provided the right training, tools, structure, incentives, and responsibilities is operational success possible. Management should ensure that skill needs are continually assessed and that the organization is able to obtain a workforce that has the required skills that match those necessary to achieve organizational goals. Training should be aimed at developing and retaining employee skill levels to meet changing organizational needs. Qualified and continuous supervision should be provided to ensure that internal control objectives are achieved. Performance evaluation and feedback, supplemented by an effective reward system, should be designed to help employees understand the connection between their performance and the organization's success. As a part of its human capital planning, management should also consider how best to retain valuable employees, plan for their eventual succession, and ensure continuity of needed skills and abilities.

GAO-12-695 Status of Recommendations

IRS's operations cover a wide range of technical activities requiring specific expertise in tax-related matters; financial management; and systems design, development, and maintenance. Because IRS has tens of thousands of employees spread throughout the country, it is imperative that management establish and maintain up-to-date guidance and provide appropriate training for its staff. Taking action to implement the following three recommendations in table 10, which are correctible in the short term, would assist IRS in its management of human capital.

Table 10: Open Recommendations to Improve IRS's Management of Human Capital

ID no.	Recommendation
07-08	Require that managers or supervisors provide the manual refund initiators in their units with training on the most current requirements to help ensure that they fulfill their responsibilities to monitor manual refunds and document their monitoring actions to prevent the issuance of duplicate refunds. (short-term)
12-19	Provide training to contracting officers and contracting officers' technical representatives (COTR) on their specific procedural requirements for obtaining and maintaining end user documentation of receipt and acceptance of the good or service prior to entering acknowledgment of receipt and acceptance in the procurement system. (short-term)
12-27	Remind managers of their responsibilities, procedures, and required time frames for either granting or denying a within-grade pay increase for employees with below fully successful ratings, such as by providing alerts in HR Connect when a manager enters a less than fully successful rating or providing training to remind them of their responsibilities. (short-term)

Source: GAO.

Concluding Observations

Increased budgetary pressures and an increased public awareness of the importance of maintaining effective accountability over trillions of dollars of tax receipts and sensitive taxpayer data have served to provide additional pressure on IRS to carry out its mission more efficiently and effectively. As such, sound financial management and effective internal controls are essential if IRS is to efficiently and effectively achieve its goals.

IRS has made substantial progress in improving its financial management and internal control since its first financial audit, as evidenced by unqualified audit opinions on its financial statements for the past 12 years, resolution of several material internal control weaknesses, significant deficiencies, and other control deficiencies, and actions taken resulting in the closure of hundreds of financial management recommendations. This progress has been the result of hard work by many individuals throughout IRS and sustained commitment of IRS leadership. Nonetheless, more needs to be done to fully address the agency's continuing financial management challenges—resolving material weaknesses and significant deficiencies in internal control; developing outcome-oriented performance metrics that can facilitate managing operations for outcomes; and correcting numerous other control deficiencies. Effective implementation of the recommendations we have made through our financial audits and related work could greatly assist IRS in improving its ability to effectively and efficiently carry out its mission.

Agency Comments and Our Evaluation

In commenting on a draft of this report, the IRS Commissioner expressed his appreciation for our acknowledgment of the agency's progress in addressing its financial management challenges as evidenced by our closure of 38 open financial management recommendations from prior GAO reports. The IRS Commissioner also stated that the agency is committed to implementing appropriate improvements to ensure that it maintains sound financial management practices. We will review the effectiveness of further corrective actions IRS has taken or will take to address all open recommendations as part of our audit of IRS's fiscal year 2012 financial statements.

We are sending copies of this report to the Chairmen and Ranking Members of the Senate Committee on Appropriations; Senate Committee on Finance; Senate Committee on Homeland Security and Governmental Affairs; and Subcommittee on Taxation, IRS Oversight and Long-Term Growth, Senate Committee on Finance. We are also sending copies to the Chairmen and Ranking Members of the House Committee on Appropriations; House Committee on Ways and Means; the Chairman and Vice Chairman of the Joint Committee on Taxation; the Secretary of the Treasury; the Acting Director of OMB; the Chairman of the IRS Oversight Board; and other interested parties. The report is also available at no charge on the GAO website at http://www.gao.gov.

If you or your staff have any questions concerning this report, please contact me at (202) 512-3406 or sebastians@gao.gov. Contact points for our Offices of Congressional Relations and Public Affairs may be found on the last page of this report. GAO staff who made major contributions to this report are listed in appendix IV.

Sincerely yours,

Steven J. Sebastian
Managing Director
Financial Management and Assurance

Appendix I: Status of GAO Recommendations from Internal Revenue Service Financial Audits and Related Management Reports

This appendix presents a summary of (1) the 77 previous GAO recommendations that were open as of the beginning of our fiscal year 2011 financial audit, (2) Internal Revenue Service (IRS) reported status and corrective actions taken or planned for such recommendations as of March 2012, and (3) our analysis of whether the control deficiencies that gave rise to the recommendations have been effectively addressed. It also includes a summary of the status of the 30 new recommendations identified as part of our fiscal year 2011 financial statement audit. Table 11 lists the recommendations by the year and recommendation number (ID no.) and also identifies the report in which the recommendation was made.

Table 11: Status of GAO Recommendations from Internal Revenue Service Financial Audits and Related Management Reports

ID no.	Recommendation	Source report	Status per IRS	Status per GAO
99-01	Manually review and eliminate duplicate or other assessments that have already been paid off to assure that all accounts related to a single assessment are appropriately credited for payments received. (short-term)	Internal Revenue Service: Immediate and Long-Term Actions Needed to Improve Financial Management (GAO/AIMD-99-16, Oct. 30, 1998), page 14.	Open. IRS continues to conduct quarterly Trust Fund Recovery Penalty (TFRP) Quality Assurance Internal Compliance Reviews (QAICR) to assess the accuracy of the TFRP accounts. IRS staff performed initial reviews of sampled cases and the results were 100 percent validated by headquarters staff. IRS used the review results to prepare quarterly and cumulative analyses of defects and error trends. Based on this, IRS (1) prepared multiple work requests to improve systemic processing on the Automated Trust Fund Recovery (ATFR) system and the Integrated Data Retrieval System (IDRS), (2) updated and clarified applicable Internal Revenue Manual (IRM) sections, (3) issued "HQ Alerts" to clarify procedures and offer advice to ATFR system users to improve the accuracy of TFRP processing, and (4) updated and significantly expanded TFRP training publications. IRS's efforts to close this recommendation are dependent upon funding for the outstanding work requests.	Open. Although IRS has made significant progress in this area, its controls remain ineffective. While IRS implemented the ATFR system, which cross-references payments received and automatically reduces the amounts owed on all related accounts when a payment is received from one related party, it is currently unable to process all payments related to such cases. ATFR can only reduce the amounts owed on all related accounts for about 56 percent of TFRP payments that it receives; the remaining ones continue to require manual processing. In 2010, IRS began conducting quarterly testing of TFRP payment processing to identify and address the root cause of errors and delays. However, IRS's actions have not been completely successful, and during our fiscal year 2011 audit we continued to find instances in which IRS did not properly record payments received on all related taxpayer accounts. We will continue to monitor IRS's actions to address this recommendation in our fiscal year 2012 audit to determine whether it (1) improves controls to ensure duplicate assessments are accurately and timely credited for all payments received and (2) identifies and corrects balances of duplicate assessments affected by IRS's failure to credit or accurately credit TFRP payments.

ID no.	Recommendation	Source report	Status per IRS	Status per GAO
01-06	Implement procedures to closely monitor the release of tax liens to ensure that they are released within 30 days of the date the related tax liability is fully satisfied. As part of these procedures, IRS should carefully analyze the causes of the delays in releasing tax liens identified by our work and prior work by IRS's former internal audit function and ensure that such procedures effectively address these issues. (short-term)	Internal Revenue Service: Recommendations to Improve Financial and Operational Management (GAO-01-42, Nov. 17, 2000), page 42.	Open. IRS continues to conduct independent semi-annual Quality Assurance internal reviews where IRS uses a cross-functional approach to examine and resolve systemic and procedural issues for any new issues found. During the year, IRS addressed several causes of late lien releases which resulted in fewer errors found than in the prior year's internal reviews. IRS will share the results of its Quality Assurance internal reviews with GAO.	Open. IRS has taken a number of actions over the years to improve its lien release processing, including the creation of a comprehensive action plan to address the various causes for lien release delays we identified, as well as those identified through its own reviews. Over the past several years, IRS has steadily completed actions on this plan and identified additional actions to improve lien release timeliness. For example, it completed various system enhancements to improve the timeliness of recognizing when a taxpayer has fully satisfied the outstanding tax liability. IRS also continues to perform targeted reviews of areas where processing delays were identified in the past. However, IRS's actions have not been fully successful in addressing this issue. During our fiscal year 2011 audit, we continued to find that IRS did not always timely release liens. In IRS's own testing of lien releases, it estimated that up to 10.3 percent of liens were not released timely. Continued weaknesses in IRS's controls over this area results in its noncompliance with Internal Revenue Code Section 6325, which requires IRS to release its tax liens within 30 days of the date the related tax liability is fully satisfied. We will continue to monitor IRS's actions to address this recommendation during our fiscal year 2012 audit.

ID no.	Recommendation	Source report	Status per IRS	Status per GAO
01-17	Develop a subsidiary ledger for leasehold improvements and implement procedures to record leasehold improvement costs as they occur. (long-term)	Internal Revenue Service: Recommendations to Improve Financial and Operational Management (GAO-01-42, Nov. 17, 2000), page 74.	Closed. Between 2001 and 2011, IRS continued to make improvements towards addressing this recommendation. IRS implemented the following procedures to record leasehold improvement costs as they occur: (1) routinely post leasehold improvement costs directly to asset accounts using the Integrated Financial System (IFS) and review monthly transactions of $50,000 and greater for all property accounts and certain expense accounts to ensure correct classification of additions, (2) maintain detailed records of asset purchases with current year asset and expense database files, and (3) track leased space and related leasehold improvements using the Electronic Project Investment Process and Graphic Database Interface system (GDI).	Closed. IRS has made progress in implementing procedures to record leasehold improvement costs as they occur. However, in lieu of developing a subsidiary ledger to determine the amount of leasehold improvement costs to post to its financial statements each year as we recommended, IRS developed a methodology to estimate the amount to post. During our fiscal year 2011 audit, we identified both limitations in the estimation methodology as well as errors in implementing the methodology. In order to provide a recommendation more closely aligned with the current status of the remaining issues to be resolved, we are closing this recommendation and have reported the remaining issues, along with a related recommendation for corrective action in our June 2012 management report. (See recommendation numbers 12-17, 12-18, and 12-19 in this report.)
05-32	Establish policies and procedures to require appropriate segregation of duties in Small Business/Self Employed (SB/SE) units of field offices with respect to preparation of Payment Posting Vouchers, Document Transmittal forms, and transmittal packages. (short-term)	Management Report: Improvements Needed in IRS's Internal Controls (GAO-05-247R, April 27, 2005), page 14.	Closed. In September 2011, IRS completed a process analysis that included analyzing the risk posed by the assignment of duties in the Collection Field function remittance process. Based on the findings of the process analysis, IRS concluded that the level of risk posed by the existing assignment of duties in the remittance process is low and acceptable.	Closed. IRS published a revision to the IRM that clarified the segregation of duties between revenue officers and clerical personnel related to payment posting vouchers, document transmittals, and transmittal packages. We verified that IRS performed a process analysis of SB/SE remittance processing practices as outlined in the IRM.

ID no.	Recommendation	Source report	Status per IRS	Status per GAO
05-33	Enforce the requirement that a document transmittal form listing the enclosed Daily Report of Collection Activity forms be included in transmittal packages, using such methods as more frequent inspections or increased reliance on error reports compiled by the service center teller units receiving the information. (short-term)	Management Report: Improvements Needed in IRS's Internal Controls (GAO-05-247R, April 27, 2005), page 14.	Open. IRS conducted its review of the Operational Review findings and the results of the review showed improvement in group manager compliance with control review requirements in all Collection areas but not to the desired level. IRS updated the IRM to further clarify the control review requirements and submitted it to be published in December 2011. IRS will do a follow-up review to ensure compliance with the IRM.	Open. IRS's actions to date have not been fully effective in addressing the issues that gave rise to this recommendation. During our fiscal year 2011 audit, we observed that clerical staff at three Small Business/Self Employed (SB/SE) offices we visited did not prepare Document Transmittal forms when transmitting multiple reports listing daily collection activity. In addition, in an internal review, IRS found that group managers did not adequately perform or document required reviews of internal control procedures for tracking and monitoring taxpayer receipts transmitted between IRS locations. We will continue to evaluate IRS's actions during our fiscal year 2012 audit.
05-38	Enforce requirements for monitoring accounts and reviewing monitoring of accounts for manual refunds. (short-term)	Management Report: Improvements Needed in IRS's Internal Controls (GAO-05-247R, April 27, 2005), page 20.	Open. IRS continues to enforce requirements to monitor accounts related to manual refunds. By March 2012, IRS will update IRM 21.4.4, Refund Inquiries, Manual Refunds, with additional guidance on required monitoring activities. IRS is also enhancing its erroneous duplicate manual refunds monthly reports to provide more detail for follow-up when erroneous refunds are identified and has automated the research portion of its monitoring process. IRS has (1) developed mandatory training for manual refund initiators and managers on creating and documenting a manual refund listing and (2) regularly reminds managers to review and document the employees' monitoring actions.	Open. During our fiscal year 2011 audit, we continued to find instances in which manual refund initiators or individuals responsible for centralized monitoring, or both, did not monitor accounts as required by the IRM, and supervisors did not verify that manual refund initiators or those responsible for centralized monitoring were following proper procedures for monitoring manual refunds. We will continue to evaluate the effectiveness of IRS's actions during our fiscal year 2012 audit.

ID no.	Recommendation	Source report	Status per IRS	Status per GAO
05-39	Enforce requirements for documenting monitoring actions and supervisory review for manual refunds. (short-term)	Management Report: Improvements Needed in IRS's Internal Controls (GAO-05-247R, April 27, 2005), page 20.	Open. IRS continues to enforce oversight of requirements to monitor manual refunds. IRS management performs weekly reviews of manual refunds to ensure employees are monitoring and documenting their reviews as required. During fiscal year 2012, IRS plans to (1) update IRM 21.4.4, Refund Inquiries, Manual Refunds, with additional guidance on required monitoring activities and (2) review IRMs service-wide to ensure they are consistent with the manual refund monitoring requirements in IRM 21.4.4.	Open. During our fiscal year 2011 audit, we continued to find instances in which manual refund initiators or individuals responsible for centralized monitoring, or both, did not monitor accounts as required by the IRM, and supervisors did not verify that manual refund initiators or those responsible for centralized monitoring were following proper procedures for monitoring manual refunds. We will continue to evaluate the effectiveness of IRS's actions during our fiscal year 2012 audit.
06-01	Require that Refund Inquiry Unit managers or supervisors document their review of all forms used to record and transmit returned refund checks prior to sending them for final processing. (short-term)	Management Report: Improvements Needed in IRS's Internal Controls (GAO-06-543R, May 12, 2006), page 5.	Closed. IRS requires all Refund Inquiry unit managers and supervisors to document their reviews of transmittal forms 3210. During site consistency reviews at two service center campuses (SCC) in June 2011 and August 2011, the Refund Inquiry team concluded that review and documentation procedures were being completed as required by IRM 1.4.16.5, Monitoring and Reviews. As of September 2011, IRS completed actions to ensure the reviews of all forms used to record and transmit returned refund checks prior to final processing had been completed.	Closed. We verified that IRS included requirements in IRM 1.4.16.5 that Refund Inquiry Unit managers document their review of all forms used to record and transmit returned refund checks prior to sending them for final processing.

ID no.	Recommendation	Source report	Status per IRS	Status per GAO
06-02	Enforce compliance with existing requirements that all IRS units transmitting taxpayer receipts and information from one IRS facility to another, including service center campuses (SCC), Taxpayer Assistance Centers (TAC), and units within the Large Business and International (LB&I) and the Tax-Exempt and Government Entities (TE/GE) business operating units, establish a system to track acknowledged copies of document transmittals. (short-term)	Management Report: Improvements Needed in IRS's Internal Controls (GAO-06-543R, May 12, 2006), page 6.	Closed. IRS has procedures in place to ensure compliance with tracking acknowledgment of document transmittals. In January 2011, IRS revised the IRM to include guidance on securing returned refund checks and to require supervisory reviews of controls over outgoing remittances. In August through December 2011, IRS conducted and documented the results of internal security reviews at all submission processing (SP) sites to determine if managerial reviews were being performed. IRS also revised the IRM to outline procedures managers must follow for maintaining the document transmittal form review log. IRS conducted nine onsite TAC reviews in fiscal year 2011 to monitor compliance with the requirements for tracking acknowledged copies of document transmittal forms. A review of the form review log itself led to including a lesson on proper completion, monitoring and tracking of the review log in the fiscal year 2012 training for applicable staff and managers. In January 2011, LB&I issued its annual executive memorandum to remind employees of their responsibility to adhere to the document transmittal procedures found in existing IRMs. TE/GE reviewed all appropriate IRM sections to ensure the IRM specifically addressed its system for tracking taxpayer remittances and the frequency and documentation to be prepared during managerial reviews. As a result, TE/GE revised several IRM sections to strengthen requirements for groups to maintain a payment/remittance logbook.	Open. IRS's actions to date have not fully addressed the issues that gave rise to our recommendation. During our fiscal year 2011 audit, we observed that two TACs' tracking of acknowledged/unacknowledged document transmittal forms was incomplete. Specifically, some acknowledged forms were not included on the Follow-up Review Log at one of those TACs and the Follow-up Review Log listed forms that were not supported by control copies. At another TAC we visited, TAC staff had not followed up on all document transmittal forms that had not been acknowledged by the Submission Processing Center within 10 days. At all eight TACs we visited, the format of the Follow-up Review Log in use was not consistent with the IRM. At two of the TACs we visited, the Follow-up Review Log was not being used to track and follow up on all transmittal forms sent from the TACs. We will continue to evaluate IRS's enforcement of existing requirements to track the transmittal of taxpayer receipts and information from one facility to another during our fiscal year 2012 audit.

ID no.	Recommendation	Source report	Status per IRS	Status per GAO
06-04	Require that managers or supervisors document their reviews of document transmittals to ensure that taxpayer receipts and/or taxpayer information mailed between IRS locations are tracked according to guidelines. (short-term)	Management Report: Improvements Needed in IRS's Internal Controls (GAO-06-543R, May 12, 2006), page 6.	Closed. IRS requires all managers and supervisors to document their review of the document transmittals used to transmit taxpayer receipts and information from one IRS facility to another. In January 2011, W&I SP updated IRM 3.8.47, Manual Deposit for Field Office Payment Processing, to include specific guidance on transmitting returned refund checks and a requirement for supervisory review of controls over outgoing remittances. In November 2010, W&I FA revised IRM 1.4.11.19.1, Maintaining Form 795A/3210 Files, to outline managerial procedures for maintaining the document transmittal form review log. FA included a lesson on proper completion, monitoring, and tracking of the transmittal form review log in its fiscal year 2012 training for FA staff and managers. In January 2011, LB&I issued its annual executive memorandum to remind employees of their responsibilities to adhere to the transmittal form procedures on tracking and monitoring returns. The memorandum also reminded managers to ensure preparation, transmittal, and tracking requirements are adhered to in the annual assurance process and oversight reviews. In November 2010, the Director, TE/GE Exempt Organizations (EO), Exam, issued a memorandum to all managers instructing them to ensure timely and accurate remittance processing. TE/GE instructed each Exam Director to obtain a copy of the operational review check-sheet used by second-level managers to document that the second-level manager checked for the existence of a transmittal form logbook and that they were reviewing it regularly. TE/GE also ensured that all Government Entities Field Group Operational Reviews included discussions on the need for retaining and reviewing the transmittal form logbooks.	Closed. IRS revised the IRM to require that TAC managers use a Follow-up Review Log to document their review of document transmittals.

ID no.	Recommendation	Source report	Status per IRS	Status per GAO
06-05	Equip all Taxpayer Assistance Centers (TAC) with adequate physical security controls to deter and prevent unauthorized access to restricted areas or office space occupied by other IRS units, including those TACs that are not scheduled to be reconfigured to the "new TAC" model in the near future. This includes appropriately separating customer service waiting areas from restricted areas in the near future by physical barriers, such as locked doors marked with signs barring entrance by unescorted customers. (short-term)	Management Report: Improvements Needed in IRS's Internal Controls (GAO-06-543R, May 12, 2006), page 8.	Open. IRS continues to identify priority locations for TAC model build out by evaluating TAC sites and customer feedback. Priority status goes to sites with security, safety and environmental health concerns. Of the 401 TAC locations, 270 have the model TAC with another 16 scheduled for completion prior to the 2012 filing season. IRS will build out all TACs in compliance with the security guidelines proposed by IRS's Physical Security and Emergency Preparedness (PSEP) office. Due to limited construction funding and complexity of scheduling, IRS cannot give definitive implementation dates for all locations. In the interim, IRS continues to use other solutions to help secure non-model TACs including theater rope or other barriers, signage, and minor alterations.	Open. IRS's efforts to address our recommendation are ongoing. Because of limited construction funding and complexity of scheduling, IRS cannot give definitive implementation dates for all locations. In the interim, IRS continues to use other solutions to help secure non-model TACs including theater rope or other barriers, signage, and minor alterations. We will continue to evaluate IRS's actions during our fiscal year 2012 audit.
07-04	Develop and implement appropriate corrective actions for any gaps in closed circuit television (CCTV) camera coverage that do not provide an unobstructed view of the entire exterior of the service center campus's (SCC) perimeter, such as adding or repositioning existing CCTV cameras or removing obstructions. (short-term)	Management Report: Improvements Needed in IRS's Internal Controls (GAO-07-689R, May 11, 2007), page 7.	Closed. IRS developed and implemented an action plan requiring all SCCs to (1) perform and validate completion of an assessment of their CCTV system to ascertain if it provided an unobstructed view of the exterior of the campus perimeter and (2) identify problems and planned corrective actions needed to mitigate any identified problems. All SCCs validated completion of the CCTV assessment and IRS identified a total of 16 problems. IRS management monitored progress and received monthly reports on the corrective actions status. All corrective actions have been addressed. Fourteen problems were corrected and management determined the remaining two met an acceptable level of risk. SCCs continue to monitor their CCTV systems to ensure an unobstructed view.	Open. IRS's actions to date have not fully addressed the issues that gave rise to our recommendation. In response to this recommendation, IRS required Territory Managers and Area Directors to validate that their SCC CCTV cameras (1) are compliant with IRM 10.2.14 (Methods of Providing Protection), (2) are not obstructed, (3) have a clear view of the entire exterior perimeter, and that (4) repairs are completed timely. However, during the validation process, IRS identified numerous gaps and/or obstacles in CCTV coverage at several of its SCCs. During our fiscal year 2011 audit, we continued to find problems with SCCs' CCTV coverage. At one of the three SCCs we visited, we found that the coverage areas for two surveillance cameras were obstructed and that one of the other cameras was not functioning properly. We will evaluate IRS's corrective actions for gaps in CCTV coverage during our fiscal year 2012 audit.

ID no.	Recommendation	Source report	Status per IRS	Status per GAO
07-08	Require that managers or supervisors provide the manual refund initiators in their units with training on the most current requirements to help ensure that they fulfill their responsibilities to monitor manual refunds and document their monitoring actions to prevent the issuance of duplicate refunds. (short-term)	Management Report: Improvements Needed in IRS's Internal Controls (GAO-07-689R, May 11, 2007), page 9.	Closed. As of December 2011, each Business Operating Division certified that all employees who initiate, approve and/or monitor manual refunds have completed the manual refund training.	Open. IRS's reported actions were completed subsequent to our fiscal year 2011 audit. We will follow up on IRS's progress in achieving the objectives of this recommendation during our fiscal year 2012 audit.
07-20	Establish and maintain sufficient secured storage space to properly secure and safeguard property and equipment inventory, including in-stock inventories, assets from incoming shipments, and assets that are in the process of being excessed or shipped out, or both. (short-term)	Management Report: Improvements Needed in IRS's Internal Controls (GAO-07-689R, May 11, 2007), page 20.	Closed. In March 2009, IRS implemented procedures for requesting secured storage space through the Employee Resource Center (ERC). Requesters initiate an ERC ticket requesting a "Property Consultation" which will engage Real Estate and Facilities Management (REFM) to work with the requester on obtaining the needed secured storage space. In October 2009, IRS published the Asset Management Policy Directive AM044 to improve the asset control procedures for all in-stock equipment to prevent the theft or loss.	Closed. IRS established procedures to ensure that sufficient secured space was available for all property and equipment not currently in use. During our fiscal year 2011 audit, we observed that IRS implemented these procedures. Specifically, we observed that there was adequate storage space and the storage areas were restricted. In addition, we observed the use of control logs to track incoming and outgoing assets.
08-06	In instances where computer programs that control penalty assessments are not functioning in accordance with the intent of the IRM, take appropriate action to correct the programs so that they function in accordance with the IRM. (long-term)	Management Report: Improvements Needed in IRS's Internal Controls (GAO-08-368R, June 4, 2008), page 10.	Open. IRS formed a cross-functional working group that continues to identify and assess penalty and interest issues. Since the group's inception, IRS has implemented programming corrections for 11 of the 19 issues. IRS tested six of these programming changes and determined that they were successful. IRS will continue to work these issues until all 19 issues are corrected.	Open. While IRS continues to complete corrective actions to address the programming issues identified from its internal review and is continuing to work on others, it has not yet completed all of its planned programming corrections. We will continue to review IRS's corrective actions to address this recommendation during our fiscal year 2012 audit.

ID no.	Recommendation	Source report	Status per IRS	Status per GAO
08-07	Develop and provide comprehensive guidance to assist Taxpayer Assistance Center (TAC) managers in conducting reviews of outlying TACs and documenting the results. This guidance should include a description of the key controls that should be in place at outlying TACs, specify how often these key controls should be reviewed, and specify how the results of each review should be documented, including follow-up on issues identified in previous TAC reviews. (short-term)	Management Report: Improvements Needed in IRS s Internal Controls (GAO-08-368R, June 4, 2008), page 11.	Closed. As of September 2011, IRS had a process in place that encompasses the key controls, requirements, field communications, and reviews to assist TAC managers reviewing outlying TACs. IRM Exhibit 1.4.11-11, Group Manager Mandatory Reviews, Reports and Certifications, documents the requirements for TAC Managers, including conducting reviews for outlying TACs. IRS sent quarterly email reminders to group managers of the requirement to complete TAC Security Remittance Review Database (TSRRD) responses. During the fiscal year 2011 Filing Season Readiness (FSR) Workshop, IRS provided a Continuing Professional Education (CPE) lesson on TSRRD reviews. Additional CPE lessons included a description and review of key controls. Group Managers completed the fiscal year 2011 FSR Workshop prior to the filing season. In addition, IRS continuously conducts TSRRD headquarters' remittance reviews and shares the results with the Area Directors. IRS used responses from the TSRRD in planning the After-Hours reviews for the first two quarters of 2011 as well as on-site physical security reviews at two locations in each area and provided the results to the Area Directors.	Closed. We verified that all of the reviews assessing controls over taxpayer receipts and information are documented in the TSRRD. IRS also stated that managers and staff were required to participate in CPE training on how to use the TSRRD and certify completion prior to filing season, and that Group Managers in place reviewed the Filing Season Readiness Workshop.

ID no.	Recommendation	Source report	Status per IRS	Status per GAO
08-12	Establish procedures to require documentation demonstrating that favorable background checks have been completed for all contractors prior to allowing them access to Taxpayer Assistance Centers (TAC) and other field offices. (short-term)	Management Report: Improvements Needed in IRS's Internal Controls (GAO-08-368R, June 4, 2008), page 16.	Closed. The General Services Administration (GSA) has taken a risk-based approach to providing background investigations for lessor personnel and contractors with routine access to Government leased space in Facility Security Level (FSL) IV Government-leased facilities or FSL III Government-leased facilities with 100 percent government occupancy. GSA stated that they were not able to provide adjudication services for their contractors in FSL I, II, and partially occupied FSL III leases. Without GSA support, IRS cannot provide background investigations, issue Personal Identity Verification cards, and meet certain security requirements. To mitigate, in May 2010, IRS issued Cleaning of Internal Revenue Space policy that prohibits the following contractors from receiving alarm codes, access cards, or keys to IRS space: cleaners, building maintenance personnel, and lessor employees. This provision prevents these individuals from accessing IRS space without employees' knowledge. IRS amended all leases to reflect the new policy.	Closed. Despite IRS's long standing efforts to work with GSA to reach an agreement to obtain documentation demonstrating favorable background checks have been completed for contractors with unescorted access to IRS space, GSA informed IRS that they were unable to provide adjudication service for contractors working in Facility Security Level I, II and partial III facilities. According to IRS, GSA has been compliant in performing background investigations for all government-owned locations, and leased facilities for Levels IV and for 100 percent occupied Level IIIs. IRS took steps to issue new guidance for facilities to enhance physical control to safeguard assets, including implementation of daytime cleaning in all leased facilities. In May 2010, IRS issued a new directive regarding the cleaning of all IRS office space stating that IRS offices will be cleaned during normal business hours only unless appropriate background investigation procedures have been completed to allow staff access. This directive set a new standard requiring, among other things, that cleaners and other building maintenance or contractor/lessor employees should not be provided access cards or keys to IRS space that would allow them access without IRS employees knowing their presence.

ID no.	Recommendation	Source report	Status per IRS	Status per GAO
08-14	Revise the IRM to include a requirement that IRS conduct periodic, unannounced inspections at off-site contractor facilities entrusted with sensitive IRS information; document the results, including identification of any security issues; and verify that the contractor has taken appropriate corrective actions on any security issues observed. (short-term)	Management Report: Improvements Needed in IRS's Internal Controls (GAO-08-368R, June 4, 2008), page 17.	Open. IRS is revising IRM 10.2.13, Information Protection, to require periodic and unannounced site inspections of IRS vendors maintaining personally identifiable information (PII), documentation of findings and follow-up to replace the interim guidance IRS issued in August 2011. In the meantime, IRS modified existing Performance Work Statements within the Sensitive Document Destruction Program to require periodic and unannounced site inspections effective February 2009. All vendors doing business under those contracts now agree to IRS periodic and unannounced site inspections of locations maintaining IRS PII for disposal purposes. To date, IRS has conducted on-site inspections of 55 vendor sites. REFM is tracking the progress of inspections to monitor coverage, as well as findings. IRS identified only minor findings that have been corrected or are in the progress of being corrected.	Open. IRS's actions to address this recommendation are ongoing. Specifically, IRS is in the process of revising the IRM to require periodic and unannounced site inspections of IRS vendors maintaining PII and documentation of the findings and follow-up. During our fiscal year 2011 audit, we found that site inspections of the off-site shredding contractor's facility servicing four of the eight field offices that we visited had not been performed. We will continue to evaluate IRS's actions during our fiscal year 2012 audit.

ID no.	Recommendation	Source report	Status per IRS	Status per GAO
08-17	Reinforce existing policies requiring IRS personnel to use the revised Form 13094 when hiring juveniles and verify the information on Form 13094 by contacting the reference directly and documenting the details of the contact. (short-term)	Management Report: Improvements Needed in IRS's Internal Controls (GAO-08-368R, June 4, 2008), page 19.	Closed. IRS has taken numerous actions to reinforce existing policies requiring verification of the information on Form 13094, Recommendation for Juvenile Employment. IRS has provided training for the (1) human resource specialists, (2) external Juvenile Program Director, (3) Senior Managers, and (4) Front Line Managers in the impacted offices. IRS implemented controls and enhanced overall program management by (1) designating a Senior Human Resource Specialist to serve as the agency wide program manager, (2) revising existing guidance to ensure dates of birth are checked, (3) revising source documents based on internal review results, and (4) requiring 100 percent validation of source documents against the internal tracking spreadsheet and Treasury Integrated Management Information System focus report that monitors juvenile hires. These controls produced error free reviews for both the third and fourth quarters of fiscal year 2011.	Closed. During our fiscal year 2011 audit, we found that IRS took corrective action to reinforce existing policies requiring verification of information on Form 13094, including contacting the reference directly and documenting the details of the contact, by: (1) conducting training for the employment offices on the use of Form 13094 and hiring juveniles, (2) developing and implementing a centralized quality review process to monitor juveniles hired, (3) implementing a centralized spreadsheet documenting all juvenile hires along with the completion of required documentation for hiring, and (4) establishing a system to maintain copies of all Form 13094s to support monthly audits.
08-24	Issue a memorandum to employees that reiterates IRS policy requiring all employees to obtain appropriate approvals of travel authorizations prior to the initiation of their travel. (short-term)	Management Report: Improvements Needed in IRS's Internal Controls (GAO-08-368R, June 4, 2008), page 25.	Closed. In seven of the last thirteen Travel Times newsletters since March 2010 and in the November 2010 issue of Leaders' Alert, IRS published reminders to travelers to file their authorizations prior to the beginning of their travel. In March 2010, Agency-Wide Shared Services (AWSS) Employee Support Services Travel Services implemented in GovTrip a system of contacting employees who are scheduled to travel within three days and whose authorization is unsigned. If the travel is still necessary, the traveler's manager must sign the authorization in GovTrip, reducing the instances of unauthorized travel.	Closed. We verified that IRS published reminders in their Travel Times newsletter and Leader' Alert notification e-mail to remind employees that they must obtain approvals on travel authorizations prior to the initiation of their travel. Furthermore, during our fiscal year 2011 audit we identified only 1 instance out of 41 travel transactions tested where the employee initiated travel prior to obtaining approval for travel.

ID no.	Recommendation	Source report	Status per IRS	Status per GAO
09-03	Document in the IRM minimum requirements for establishing criteria for time discrepancies or other inconsistencies, which if noted as part of the required monitoring of Form 10160, Receipt for Transport of IRS Deposit, would require off-site surveillance of couriers. (short-term)	Management Report: Improvements Are Needed to Enhance IRS's Internal Controls and Operating Effectiveness (GAO-09-513R, June 24, 2009), page 10.	Closed. In April 2011, IRS updated the Statements of Work for all submission Processing sites. Updates reflect the new timeframes that courier service contractors must follow when delivering deposits to the financial institution. The new timeframes allow for courier service deliveries to be made in a safe and responsible manner while ensuring that the deposit will be delivered with no unauthorized stops. In April 2011, IRS updated IRM 3.8.45, Deposit Activity—Manual Deposit Process, to reflect responsibilities of Submission Processing Receipt & Control Operations Managers, Contracting Officer Technical Representatives, and Headquarters Analysts for monitoring Form 10160, Receipt for Transport of IRS Deposit, and actions to take when they find inconsistencies in reported time.	Open. IRS's actions to date have not been effective in addressing the intent of this recommendation. We reviewed the updated IRM 3.8.45 and found that IRS did not document criteria that established what should be considered as time discrepancies or other inconsistencies. We will continue to evaluate IRS's efforts to monitor courier activities during our fiscal year 2012 audit.
09-04	Document in the IRM minimum requirements for conducting off-site surveillance of couriers entrusted with taxpayer receipts and information. (short-term)	Management Report: Improvements Are Needed to Enhance IRS's Internal Controls and Operating Effectiveness (GAO-09-513R, June 24, 2009), page 10.	Closed. In April 2011, IRS updated the Statements of Work for all Submission Processing sites as well as IRM 3.8.45.1.9.7(3), Headquarters Deposit Analyst Responsibility, to identify the minimum requirement that headquarters deposit analysts will conduct courier surveillance during unannounced security reviews. The IRM update also states that timeframes for courier delivery of deposits listed in the courier contract Statement of Work will be reassessed during the unannounced internal security reviews by headquarters analysts or whenever the depository location changes.	Closed. In April 2011, IRS updated the Statement of Work (SOW), as well as IRM 3.8.45.1.9.7(3), "Headquarters Deposit Analyst Responsibility," outlining the minimum requirement that headquarters analysts will conduct courier surveillance during unannounced security reviews. The IRM update also states the time frames for courier delivery of deposits listed in the courier contract SOW will be reassessed during the unannounced internal security reviews by headquarters analysts or whenever the depository location changes.
09-05	Establish procedures to track and routinely report the total dollar amounts and volumes of receipts collected by individual Taxpayer Assistance Center (TAC) location, group, territory, area, and nationwide. (long-term)	Management Report: Improvements Are Needed to Enhance IRS's Internal Controls and Operating Effectiveness (GAO-09-513R, June 24, 2009), page 11.	Open. IRS is currently testing an electronic Form 795A, Remittance and Return Report, to track and report the total dollar amounts and volumes of receipts. IRS will mandate use of the revised form to collect and report data at the Taxpayer Assistance Center level once testing is completed, which is anticipated to be October 2012.	Open. IRS's efforts to address our recommendation are ongoing. We will continue to evaluate IRS's actions during our fiscal year 2012 audit.

ID no.	Recommendation	Source report	Status per IRS	Status per GAO
09-06	Establish procedures to ensure that an inventory of all duress alarms is documented for each location and is readily available to individuals conducting duress alarm tests before each test is conducted. (short-term)	Management Report: Improvements Are Needed to Enhance IRS's Internal Controls and Operating Effectiveness (GAO-09-513R, June 24, 2009), page 13.	Open. In October 2011, IRS convened a development team to improve the alarm testing and reporting process. IRS will pilot test an Alarm Testing Form to document testing of the duress alarms at each facility. The form will list each alarm at the facility, the status of the alarm test and, where necessary, any corrective action taken. This will provide an update to the alarm inventory each time the alarms are tested. IRS expects to finalize the form along with a related Standard Operating Procedure for use by each territory office in fiscal year 2012.	Open. IRS revised its IRM to require a readily available inventory of all duress alarms for individuals conducting the alarm tests; however, these actions have not been fully effective in addressing the issues that gave rise to this recommendation. During our fiscal year 2011 audit, an inventory of all duress alarms was not readily available to individuals conducting duress alarm testing at four of the eight field offices we visited. We will continue to evaluate IRS's actions during our fiscal year 2012 audit.
09-07	Establish procedures to periodically update the inventory of duress alarms at each Taxpayer Assistance Center (TAC) location to ensure that the inventory is current and complete as of the testing date. (short-term)	Management Report: Improvements Are Needed to Enhance IRS's Internal Controls and Operating Effectiveness (GAO-09-513R, June 24, 2009), page 13.	Open. As noted in the response to recommendation 09-06 above, IRS will develop an Alarm Testing Form that lists each of the duress alarms and will make it available to any employee who needs it for additional testing, planning future testing or validating the alarm inventory.	Open. IRS's actions to date have not been fully effective in addressing the issues that gave rise to this recommendation. During our fiscal year 2011 audit, duress alarm testing at seven of the eight TACs we visited did not include a documented quarterly validation of the duress alarm inventory signed and dated by a PSEP official. Additionally, at one of the TACs we visited, unused mobile duress alarms that were included on the alarm inventory were not being tested. We will continue to evaluate IRS's actions during our fiscal year 2012 audit.
09-08	Provide instructions for conducting quarterly duress alarm tests to ensure that IRS officials conducting the test (1) document the test results for each duress alarm listed in the inventory, including date, findings, and planned corrective action and (2) track the findings until they are properly resolved. (short-term)	Management Report: Improvements Are Needed to Enhance IRS's Internal Controls and Operating Effectiveness (GAO-09-513R, June 24, 2009), page 13.	Open. As noted in the response to recommendation 09-06 above, IRS will publish a standard operating procedure along with the issuance of the Alarm Testing Form. The procedure will provide recommended steps for conducting the alarm tests. The steps may vary due to differing conditions or processes in each territory office or in the office being tested, but once the form is finalized and adopted, it will be the standard for testing duress alarms regardless of local conditions.	Open. IRS's actions to date have not been fully effective in addressing the issues that gave rise to this recommendation. During our fiscal year 2011 audit, non-TAC duress alarms were not tested on a quarterly basis at seven of the eight field offices we visited. Additionally, at three of the field offices we visited, local instructions (i.e., Standard Operating Procedures [SOP]), outlining necessary steps for properly completing duress alarm tests, were not provided to the individual(s) performing the duress alarm testing. We will continue to evaluate IRS's actions during our fiscal year 2012 audit.

ID no.	Recommendation	Source report	Status per IRS	Status per GAO
09-09	Establish procedures requiring that each physical security analyst conduct a periodic documented review of the Emergency Signal History Report and emergency contact list for its respective location to ensure that (1) appropriate corrective actions have been planned for all incidents reported by the central monitoring station and (2) the emergency contact list for each location is current and includes only appropriate contacts. (short-term)	Management Report: Improvements Are Needed to Enhance IRS's Internal Controls and Operating Effectiveness (GAO-09-513R, June 24, 2009), page 13.	Closed. Beginning in January 2012, IRS will transmit daily all Events History Reports to each territory manager for the accounts or facilities in their territory. This will allow the territory specialist to review the alarm events on a daily basis. While the requirement for quarterly certification remains, daily reviews will allow for more immediate investigation and resolution of events considered to be out of the ordinary.	Open. The procedures that IRS established during fiscal year 2011 in this area have not been fully effective in addressing the issues that gave rise to this recommendation. At all eight field offices that we visited, a quarterly review of the Emergency Signal History Report to ensure that appropriate corrective actions have been planned for all deficiencies or incidents requiring actions reported by the central monitoring station was not performed, documented, dated, or signed by a PSEP representative. Additionally, at seven of the field offices we visited, an appropriately qualified individual was not listed as the designated first responder during business hours on the duress alarm contact list. The procedures IRS implemented in January 2012 occurred subsequent to our fiscal year 2011 audit. We will continue to evaluate IRS's actions during our fiscal year 2012 audit.
09-16	Develop outcome-oriented performance measures and related performance goals for IRS's enforcement programs and activities that include measures of the full cost of, and the revenue collected from, those programs and activities (return on investment) to assist IRS's managers in optimizing resource allocation decisions and evaluating the effectiveness of their activities. (long-term)	Management Report: Improvements Are Needed to Enhance IRS's Internal Controls and Operating Effectiveness (GAO-09-513R, June 24, 2009), page 25.	Closed. IRS has updated and expanded the existing portfolio of cost studies, which include several outcome-oriented performance measures. As part of that effort, an additional cost study was developed on the cost/benefit of Balance Due Notices. IRS is continuing to work with its Business Units to expand the use of notice data information and cost information to determine the efficiency of notices. IRS has also been working to improve the methodology for the cost of the different types of Correspondence and Field exams. This methodology will enable cost to be calculated at a lower level of detail within these areas. Senior management within IRS will continue to look into integrating the information into the management processes and performance metrics at each business unit.	Open. IRS has updated and expanded the existing portfolio of cost studies, which include several outcome-oriented performance measures. During fiscal year 2011, some of IRS's business operating units had begun to implement aspects of performance measurement into their decision making processes. However, such progress has not yet extended to IRS's primary business unit responsible for developing and directing IRS's corporate-wide enforcement programs and activities to collect unpaid taxes, about which our recommendation is focused. We will continue to evaluate IRS's actions to develop and implement performance measures for its enforcement programs and activities during our fiscal year 2012 audit.

ID no.	Recommendation	Source report	Status per IRS	Status per GAO
10-01	Review the results of IRS's unpaid assessments compensating statistical estimation process to identify and document instances where systemic limitations in the Custodial Detail Data Base (CDDB) resulted in misclassifications of account balances that, in turn, resulted in material inaccuracies in the amounts of reported unpaid assessments. (short-term)	Management Report: Improvements Are Needed in IRS's Internal Controls and Compliance with Laws and Regulations (GAO-10-565R, June 28, 2010), page 10.	Open. IRS has an established process in place to annually review the identified errors on the sampled cases selected for the unpaid assessment statistical estimation process to identify where misclassifications of account balances were caused by systemic limitations in CDDB. In November 2011, IRS completed its review and identified programming changes to improve the business rules used by CDDB to accurately classify unpaid tax assessments.	Open. During our fiscal year 2011 audit, we and IRS continued to identify misclassified unpaid assessments account modules resulting from CDDB systemic limitations. As part of its unpaid assessments estimation process, IRS identified 27 cases in its taxes receivable sample that were either misclassified in whole or in part due to CDDB systemic limitations and recorded adjustments to these accounts to reflect the correct classification or value at the point in time that IRS sampled the account information. On the basis of a statistical projection of these and other individual adjustments, IRS had to make a multibillion dollar adjustment to the year-end balance of gross taxes receivable generated by CDDB in order to produce a reliable taxes receivable balance for external reporting on its balance sheet for fiscal year 2011. While IRS identified and documented specific account modules that were misclassified as a result of systemic limitations, it has not compiled a listing of these systemic limitations in order to track and monitor the status of programming changes aimed at addressing these limitations. We will continue to monitor IRS's actions to address this recommendation during our fiscal year 2012 audit.
10-02	Research and implement programming changes to allow CDDB to more accurately classify such accounts among the three categories of unpaid tax assessments. (short-term)	Management Report: Improvements Are Needed in IRS's Internal Controls and Compliance with Laws and Regulations (GAO-10-565R, June 28, 2010), page 10.	Open. In November 2011, IRS requested programming changes in CDDB to accurately classify unpaid tax assessments, including modules for individuals with split classifications between taxes receivable, compliance assessments, and Memo. These changes are scheduled to be implemented in June 2012.	Open. IRS is in the process of implementing numerous programming changes to improve CDDB's accuracy in classifying accounts among the three categories of unpaid tax assessments. We will continue to monitor IRS's corrective actions to address this recommendation as part of our fiscal year 2012 audit.

ID no.	Recommendation	Source report	Status per IRS	Status per GAO
10-03	Research and identify control weaknesses resulting in inaccuracies or errors in taxpayer accounts that materially affect the financial reporting of unpaid tax assessments. (short-term)	Management Report: Improvements Are Needed in IRS's Internal Controls and Compliance with Laws and Regulations (GAO-10-565R, June 28, 2010), page 10.	Open. IRS has an established process in place to annually review the identified errors on the sampled and unsampled cases selected for the unpaid assessment statistical estimation process, and the IRM procedures to ensure proper internal controls are in place to avoid future errors. In November 2011, IRS completed the fiscal year 2011 review and continued to identify misclassifications of account balances requiring corrections. IRS distributed this report to its Business Operating Divisions to take appropriate corrective actions. IRS is looking at ways to identify control weaknesses and inaccuracies in taxpayer accounts that materially affect the financial reporting of unpaid tax assessments for other than sampled cases.	Open. During our fiscal year 2011 audit, we and IRS continued to identify misclassified unpaid assessments accounts resulting from IRS processing errors or delays. As part of its unpaid assessments estimation process, IRS identified 12 cases in its taxes receivable sample that were misclassified in whole or in part due to errors in the taxpayer accounts, and recorded adjustments to these accounts to reflect the correct classification or value at the point in time that IRS sampled the account information. On the basis of a statistical projection of these and other individual adjustments, IRS had to make a multibillion dollar adjustment to the year-end balance of gross taxes receivable generated by CDDB in order to produce a reliable taxes receivable balance for external reporting on its balance sheet for fiscal year 2011. While IRS compiled a report listing the errors identified in its unpaid assessment estimation process and attempted to identify the IRS unit where the error occurred, IRS did not identify the underlying control deficiencies that resulted in the errors or delays. IRS cannot implement appropriate corrective actions unless it identifies the specific control deficiency or deficiencies that resulted in the errors or delays. We will monitor IRS's actions during our fiscal year 2012 audit to determine whether it is identifying the underlying control weaknesses that result in inaccuracies or errors in taxpayer accounts that materially affect its financial reporting of unpaid tax assessments.

ID no.	Recommendation	Source report	Status per IRS	Status per GAO
10-04	Once IRS identifies the control weaknesses that result in inaccuracies or errors that materially affect the financial reporting of unpaid tax assessments, implement control procedures to routinely prevent, or to detect and correct, such errors. (short-term)	Management Report: Improvements Are Needed in IRS's Internal Controls and Compliance with Laws and Regulations (GAO-10-565R, June 28, 2010), page 10.	Open. In November 2011, IRS distributed the annual report with the identified errors to the Business Operating divisions (BODs) for corrective actions, and revisions to IRM procedures where necessary. The BODs are required to provide an annual status of the corrective actions taken. IRS will continue to identify and validate corrective actions that were completed. IRS will continue to monitor appropriate procedures, controls, and program modifications.	Open. During our fiscal year 2011 audit, we and IRS continued to identify misclassified unpaid assessments accounts resulting from IRS processing errors or delays. As part of its unpaid assessments estimation process, IRS identified 12 cases in its taxes receivable sample that were misclassified in whole or in part due to errors in the taxpayer accounts, and recorded adjustments to these accounts to reflect the correct classification or value at the point in time that IRS sampled the account information. On the basis of a statistical projection of these and other individual adjustments, IRS had to make a multibillion dollar adjustment to the year-end balance of gross taxes receivable generated by CDDB in order to produce a reliable taxes receivable balance for external reporting on its balance sheet for fiscal year 2011. While IRS compiled a report listing the errors identified in its unpaid assessment estimation process and attempted to identify the IRS unit where the error occurred, IRS did not implement corrective actions to routinely prevent, or detect and correct similar errors in taxpayer accounts. We will monitor IRS's actions during our fiscal year 2012 audit to determine whether IRS implements appropriate corrective actions to routinely prevent, or detect and correct, errors in taxpayer accounts.

ID no.	Recommendation	Source report	Status per IRS	Status per GAO
10-05	Revise the IRM to provide specific requirements for supervisors to review the accuracy of credit transactions related to Trust Fund Recovery Penalty (TFRP) payments processed through the Automated Trust Fund Recovery (ATFR) system. This guidance should provide specific areas to review and list the ATFR system reports that can facilitate supervisory reviews. (short-term)	Management Report: Improvements Are Needed in IRS's Internal Controls and Compliance with Laws and Regulations (GAO-10-565R, June 28, 2010), page 15.	Closed. In November 2011, IRS published a new IRM 5.19.14 on TFRPs that includes requirement 5.19.14.5 (3), Manager Reports, that supervisors review 100 percent of the payment cross-references prior to account posting.	Closed. We verified that IRS revised the IRM to provide specific requirements for supervisors to review the accuracy of credit transactions related to TFRP payments processed through the ATFR system.
10-06	Formalize and implement the quarterly reviews of Trust Fund Recovery Penalty (TFRP) payment transactions to monitor compliance with the IRM requirements. (short-term)	Management Report: Improvements Are Needed in IRS's Internal Controls and Compliance with Laws and Regulations (GAO-10-565R, June 28, 2010), page 15.	Closed. In March, June, September and December 2011, IRS conducted its quarterly Quality Assurance Internal Compliance Review process and monitored compliance with IRM requirements by reviewing a statistically valid sample of payments and credits that it selected from a Master File extract for the specified periods of time. IRS also incorporated the quarterly review process in its Standard Operating Procedures, Trust Fund Recovery Penalty Quality Assurance Internal Compliance Review, published in December 2011.	Closed. We verified that IRS formalized and implemented quarterly reviews of TFRP payment transactions to monitor compliance with the IRM requirements.
10-07	Develop procedures to analyze the results of the quarterly reviews of TFRP payment transactions so that specific factors causing the errors are identified. (short-term)	Management Report: Improvements Are Needed in IRS's Internal Controls and Compliance with Laws and Regulations (GAO-10-565R, June 28, 2010), page 15.	Closed. In December 2011, IRS completed its formal Standard Operating Procedures for both Campus and Headquarters to identify and analyze error trends based on the findings from each quarterly review and the cumulative review results. IRS continues to monitor the results of quarterly reviews.	Closed. We verified that IRS developed procedures to analyze the results of its quarterly TFRP payment transaction reviews to identify specific factors causing errors.

ID no.	Recommendation	Source report	Status per IRS	Status per GAO
10-08	Develop procedures to address the factors causing errors in the processing of TFRP payment transactions identified through the analyses of the quarterly review results. (short-term)	Management Report: Improvements Are Needed in IRS's Internal Controls and Compliance with Laws and Regulations (GAO-10-565R, June 28, 2010), page 15.	Closed. In 2011, IRS analyzed the results from its quarterly reviews of TFRP payment transactions and developed various procedures to address the factors causing errors. IRS's actions included updating its IRM and initiating programming changes to its ATFR system. IRS continues to monitor and analyze the results of its quarterly TFRP payment reviews to identify the root cause of processing errors.	Closed. We verified that IRS developed procedures to address the factors causing errors in the processing of TFRP payment transactions.
10-15	Revise the IRM to require IRS's Central Insolvency Operation (CIO) to timely provide service center campuses (SCC) an acknowledgment of receipt for each Form 3210 transmittal related to a duplicate refund transcript sent to them by an SCC for review. (short-term)	Management Report: Improvements Are Needed in IRS's Internal Controls and Compliance with Laws and Regulations (GAO-10-565R, June 28, 2010), page 21.	Closed. In April 2011, IRS revised the IRM to include a provision that requires receipt acknowledgments for Form 3210 to be returned timely to the originator.	Closed. We verified that IRS revised the IRM to include procedures for CIO to timely provide acknowledgment of receipt for Form 3210 related to duplicate refund transcripts to the SCCs.
10-16	Revise the IRM to require service center campuses (SCC) to verify that an acknowledgment of receipt has been received from IRS's Central Insolvency Operation (CIO) for 100 percent of the Form 3210 transmittals related to duplicate refund transcripts that have been forwarded to CIO for review. (short-term)	Management Report: Improvements Are Needed in IRS's Internal Controls and Compliance with Laws and Regulations (GAO-10-565R, June 28, 2010), page 21.	Closed. In January 2011, IRS updated the table in IRM 3.17.79.4.1.2, Duplicate Refund Transcript, to instruct accounting employees to route duplicate refund transcripts to the required function within 24 to 48 hours of review and to verify acknowledgment of receipt. IRS will be ensuring compliance with the successful acknowledgments of the 3210s and will have quarterly statistics available in May 2012.	Closed. We verified that IRS revised the IRM to include procedures for verifying acknowledgments received from CIO for duplicate refund transcripts at SCCs.
10-17	Revise the IRM to require service center campuses (SCC) to resolve any instances in which an acknowledgment of receipt for a Form 3210 transmittal related to duplicate refund transcripts is not received. (short-term)	Management Report: Improvements Are Needed in IRS's Internal Controls and Compliance with Laws and Regulations (GAO-10-565R, June 28, 2010), page 21.	Closed. In November 2011, IRS updated IRM 3.17.79.4.1.2, Duplicate Refund Transcript, to instruct employees on actions to take when a Form 3210 has not been acknowledged by the CIO function.	Closed. We verified that IRS revised the IRM to include procedures to resolve instances in which acknowledgment of receipt for a Form 3210 has not been received.

ID no.	Recommendation	Source report	Status per IRS	Status per GAO
10-18	Require service center campuses (SCC) to acknowledge unprocessable items with receipts received from lockbox banks. (short-term)	Management Report: Improvements Are Needed in IRS's Internal Controls and Compliance with Laws and Regulations (GAO-10-565R, June 28, 2010), page 23.	Closed. In January 2011, IRS published IRM 3.10.73, Campus Mail and Work Control—Batching and Numbering, and IRM 3.8.44, Deposit Activity—Campus Deposit Activity, to include the requirement for service center campuses to acknowledge unprocessable items with receipts received from lockbox banks. Submission Processing Centers (SPC) are required to fax the Lockbox Document Transmittal (LDT) form daily to the lockbox bank. SPC receiving areas perform daily LDT reviews and track discrepancies on a Lockbox Performance Measures Data Collection Instrument. Lockbox Field Coordinators (LFC) conduct on-site lockbox bank reviews as part of the Processing Internal Control review. These on-site reviews track and record whether the center is completing LDT acknowledgments correctly and if internal controls are in place to ensure documents are returned from the SPC to the bank daily. The LFCs then retain copies of the LDTs and sign acknowledgments.	Closed. We verified that IRS updated the IRM and the Lockbox Document Transmittal form instructions to require SCCs to acknowledge unprocessable items with receipts received from lockbox banks.
10-19	Establish procedures to track service center campus (SCC) acknowledgments of unprocessable items with receipts. (short-term)	Management Report: Improvements Are Needed in IRS's Internal Controls and Compliance with Laws and Regulations (GAO-10-565R, June 28, 2010), page 23.	Closed. In January 2011, IRS published IRM 3.10.73, Campus Mail and Work Control—Batching and Numbering, and IRM 3.8.44, Deposit Activity—Campus Deposit Activity, to require IRS to track service center campuses acknowledgments for unprocessable items with receipts. In addition, Submission Processing (SP) Lockbox established procedures to track service center campus acknowledgments of unprocessable items. SP receiving areas responsible for returning the LDT daily to the banks perform daily reviews. In December 2011, SP developed a process to track the daily submission of the LDT acknowledgments back to the banks.	Open. Although IRS implemented procedures in the IRM for service center personnel to track acknowledgments for unprocessable items with receipts, the updates do not include procedures for lockbox banks to track whether service centers are timely acknowledging the receipt of unprocessable items. We will continue to evaluate IRS's efforts to establish procedures for lockbox banks to track whether service centers are timely acknowledging the receipt of unprocessable items during our fiscal year 2012 audit.

ID no.	Recommendation	Source report	Status per IRS	Status per GAO
10-20	Establish procedures to monitor the process used by service center campuses (SCC) and lockbox banks to acknowledge and track transmittals of unprocessable items with receipts. These procedures should include monitoring discrepancies and instituting appropriate corrective actions as needed. (short-term)	Management Report: Improvements Are Needed in IRS's Internal Controls and Compliance with Laws and Regulations (GAO-10-565R, June 28, 2010), page 23.	Closed. IRS developed, and provided detailed instructions for the preparation and verification of, the Lockbox Document Transmittal (LDT) form to Lockbox banks and Submission Processing Centers (SPC). These procedures were incorporated into IRM sections in January 2011. In fiscal year 2011, SPCs conducted daily reviews that showed minor remittance count discrepancies at most lockbox banks, but overall they showed improvement in package mail-out preparation and addressing the LDT Listing of items remitted with the receipts that the lockbox cannot process. LFCs also conducted on-site lockbox bank reviews as part of the Processing Internal Control Performance Measure Reviews. These on-site reviews track and record whether the center is completing LDT acknowledgments correctly and if internal controls are in place to ensure documents are returned from the SPC to the bank daily. The LFCs then retain copies of the LDTs and sign acknowledgments. In fiscal year 2011, on-site lockbox bank reviews indicated that all required Internal Control Reviews related to LDT preparation, acknowledgment, and retention, were met. LFCs provide additional training and clarification to banks and SPCs that have difficulty meeting guidance or have higher error rates.	Open. IRS has not yet demonstrated whether its procedures are effectively designed. IRS designed procedures to monitor this process that would be undertaken by Lockbox Field Coordinators (LFC) during their routine on-site quality reviews, which have been conducted quarterly. However, IRS has reduced the frequency of those quality reviews to an annual review during fiscal year 2012. We will evaluate the effect of this frequency decrease during our fiscal year 2012 audit to determine if IRS's procedures provide adequate monitoring of the process.

ID no.	Recommendation	Source report	Status per IRS	Status per GAO
10-26	Review the Taxpayer Assistance Center Security and Remittance Review Database (TSRRD) for clarity and revise review questions as appropriate. (short-term)	Management Report: Improvements Are Needed in IRS's Internal Controls and Compliance with Laws and Regulations (GAO-10-565R, June 28, 2010), page 28.	Closed. In January 2011, IRS reviewed the TSRRD and revised the questions for clarification. IRM Exhibit 1.4.11-15, Taxpayer Assistance Center/Payment Processing Checklist, revised in January 2011, now reflects the revised TSRRD remittance questions. In addition, IRS continued to provide training that emphasized when and how the key controls should be reviewed. IRS also continued the headquarters-led TSRRD remittance reviews and is sharing the results with the Area Directors.	Closed. We verified that IRS reviewed the TSRRD questions for clarity and as a result revised several of them in January 2011.
10-27	Provide training to Taxpayer Assistance Center (TAC) group managers to assist with their understanding of the TAC Security and Remittance Review Database (TSRRD) review questions and related objectives. This training should be provided on an ongoing basis to account for changes in TSRRD questions and for newly hired or appointed TAC group managers. (short-term)	Management Report: Improvements Are Needed in IRS's Internal Controls and Compliance with Laws and Regulations (GAO-10-565R June 28, 2010), page 28.	Closed. IRS continues to provide training to help TAC Group Managers execute their responsibilities regarding the TSRRD. The 2011 Filing Season Readiness (FSR) training contained two lessons for Group Manager reviews of remittance and data security; one on Payment Processing Reviews and the other on Understanding TSRRD Reviews. By January 2011, Group Managers reviewed the FSR Workshop and certified their completion of the training. The fiscal year 2011 training materials are available at the group level for managers to review. The fiscal year 2012 training will be delivered during the first quarter to frontline and administrative employees and includes a lesson on Form 795/3210 and the proper completion, monitoring and tracking of the 795/3210 review log. Field Assistance continues to focus on issues arising from TSRRD reviews.	Closed. IRS included guidance on how to use the TSRRD in the 2010 and 2011 Filing Season Readiness Workshop and TAC managers certified to their Territory Managers on January 14, 2011, that they had completed this training. In addition, we did not identify any TAC managers during our fiscal year 2011 internal control testing visits who had not received this training.

ID no.	Recommendation	Source report	Status per IRS	Status per GAO
10-29	Analyze the various contractor access arrangements and establish a policy that requires security awareness training for all IRS contractors who are provided unescorted physical access to its facilities or taxpayer receipts and information. (short-term)	Management Report: Improvements Are Needed in IRS's Internal Controls and Compliance with Laws and Regulations (GAO-10-565R, June 28, 2010), page 29.	Open. In December 2011, IRS performed an assessment of the existing contractor access arrangements to determine whether medical, cafeteria, landscaping, janitorial, building maintenance and other repair maintenance personnel should be required to take security awareness training, and if so, what the content should include. The assessment resulted in recommendations for future actions to mitigate risks associated with inadvertent access to sensitive but unclassified (SBU) data. By January 2012, IRS will finalize decisions that will include implementing a new training module to mitigate risks associated with inadvertent access to SBU data in buildings that have exemptions to the clean desk policy. The training will be delivered on or after July 2012.	Open. IRS's actions to date have not been fully effective in addressing the issues that gave rise to this recommendation. Specifically, at four of the eight field offices and two of the three SCCs we visited, contractors with staff-like access to IRS space did not receive security awareness training covering (1) authorized and unauthorized disclosures of taxpayer information, (2) basic protection policies concerning taxpayer receipts and information, and (3) federal penalties for not protecting this information. We will continue to evaluate IRS's actions during our fiscal year 2012 audit.
10-30	Designate management responsibility and establish a process for monitoring compliance with and enforcing the IRM requirement for all service center campus (SCC) Unit Security Representatives (USR) to complete (1) the required initial USR training prior to assuming their responsibilities, and (2) annual refresher training each year thereafter. (short-term)	Management Report: Improvements Are Needed in IRS's Internal Controls and Compliance with Laws and Regulations (GAO-10-565R, June 28, 2010), page 31.	Closed. In December 2010, IRS designated management responsibility and established a process for monitoring compliance with and enforcing the IRM training requirement for all service center campus USRs. IRS completed its review of the initial and refresher USR training course content and implemented a revised refresher course on the Enterprise Learning Management System for all USRs. IRS also developed and implemented a reporting capability to identify USRs that fail to comply with the initial and annual training requirements. In January 2011, IRS began distributing the monthly reports on non-compliance to the USR managers.	Closed. We verified that IRS established a process for monitoring compliance with USR training requirements and designated management to enforce compliance.
10-32	Establish a process to periodically review and update service center campus (SCC) Unit Security Representatives (USR) training materials as appropriate. (short-term)	Management Report: Improvements Are Needed in IRS's Internal Controls and Compliance with Laws and Regulations (GAO-10-565R, June 28, 2010), page 31.	Closed. IRS performs a review of USR training courses at least annually and, if required, updates the training course and materials. In December 2010, IRS completed its review of the initial and refresher USR training course content and implemented a revised refresher course on the Enterprise Learning Management System for all USRs.	Closed. We verified that IRS included language in the IRM that requires review of the USR training materials at least annually by the end of each calendar year to ensure they reflect current security policies and procedures.

ID no.	Recommendation	Source report	Status per IRS	Status per GAO
10-33	Establish procedures requiring the Director of IRS's Human Capital Office, Leadership, Education and Delivery Services (HCO LEADS) or designee to periodically monitor each business unit's progress in complying with mandatory briefing requirements. (short-term)	Management Report: Improvements Are Needed in IRS s Internal Controls and Compliance with Laws and Regulations (GAO-10-565R, June 28, 2010), page 33.	Closed. IRS HCO established procedures for business units to monitor progress in complying with mandatory briefing requirements. In August 2011 these procedures were distributed by e-mail to all embedded Human Resource directors, their points of contact, and subsequently posted on the Mandatory Briefing website. By October 2011, HCO implemented all reports to monitor the progress of employee completion of the mandatory briefing requirements. HCO runs weekly reports during the mandatory briefing cycle to obtain the status for existing employees and quarterly reports thereafter, and runs quarterly reports to obtain the status for new employees. HCO provides the reports electronically to the business units with instructions to monitor completion of the briefings and follow up as needed. HCO LEADS monitors the reports to ensure that business units are making progress in completing their briefings.	Closed. We verified that IRS has established procedures for business units to monitor their progress in complying with mandatory briefing requirements. In addition, we verified that in fiscal year 2011, IRS distributed various completion statistics of mandatory briefing requirements to designated business unit points of contact, including Human Resource directors.
11-01	Put procedures in place to periodically monitor the effectiveness of the new First-time Homebuyer Credit (FTHBC) validity checks for the duration of the filing of FTHBC claims to verify that they are working as intended. (short-term)	Management Report: Improvements Are Needed to Enhance Internal Revenue Service's Internal Controls and Operating Effectiveness (GAO-11-494R, June 21, 2011), page 9.	Open. IRS continued monitoring the effectiveness of return processing validity checks and controls, including FTHBC claims. IRS continues to review and resolve the unpostable code reports daily to monitor the effectiveness of return processing validity checks.	Open. We will continue to evaluate the effectiveness of IRS's ongoing efforts to address this recommendation during our fiscal year 2012 audit.

ID no.	Recommendation	Source report	Status per IRS	Status per GAO
11-02	Establish a mechanism to enforce the existing requirement for appropriate managers to immediately notify the manual refund units of any personnel changes affecting the approval or processing of manual refunds. This may be accomplished through mechanisms such as issuing periodic alerts, providing training or having the manual refund unit perform quarterly validations of the list of manual refund approving officials, or a combination of these. (short-term)	Management Report: Improvements Are Needed to Enhance Internal Revenue Service's Internal Controls and Operating Effectiveness (GAO-11-494R, June 21, 2011), page 10.	Closed. In August 2011, IRS incorporated a procedural change into the IRM that requires all Service Center Accounting functions to provide a list of manual refund authorizers to the Head of Office in each Business Operating Division to validate individuals who are still authorized to sign manual refunds. This listing will be required on a quarterly basis starting at the end of January 2012.	Open. The steps IRS has taken to address the issues related to this recommendation were implemented after our fiscal year 2011 audit's completion. We will evaluate the effectiveness of IRS's corrective actions to address this recommendation during our fiscal year 2012 audit.
11-03	Send out a reminder to all staff to follow policies and procedures for obtaining approval and funding of proposed purchases prior to entering into an agreement with vendors. (short-term)	Management Report: Improvements Are Needed to Enhance Internal Revenue Service's Internal Controls and Operating Effectiveness (GAO-11-494R, June 21, 2011), page 13.	Closed. In August 2011, IRS sent a reminder to all employees to follow policies and procedures for obtaining approval and funding of proposed purchases prior to entering into an agreement with vendors. IRS also placed the reminder on the IRS Intranet site.	Closed. During our fiscal year 2011 audit, we verified that IRS sent out a reminder to staff to obtain approval and funding prior to entering into an agreement with vendors. Furthermore, we did not identify any instances in which IRS entered into an agreement without first obtaining approval and funding for the purchase during our detailed testing of fiscal year 2011 nonpayroll expenses.
11-04	Establish formal written procedures requiring staff to review purchase contract terms against the goods and services received to date before requesting additional goods or services. (short-term)	Management Report: Improvements Are Needed to Enhance Internal Revenue Service's Internal Controls and Operating Effectiveness (GAO-11-494R, June 21, 2011), page 13.	Closed. In June 2011, IRS updated its Office of Procurement web site to address the requirement to (1) review contract terms and status of deliverables and (2) ensure that all related ordering activity is in compliance with the terms and conditions of the contract. The web site was developed as on online tool to assist the business operating divisions with guidance on the procurement process. It is intended to be used as supplemental information to the policy framework and provides another tool for IRS employees to navigate the procurement process.	Open. During our fiscal year 2011 audit, we verified that IRS updated the reference guide on the office of procurement's website; however, the update did not explicitly require a review of the contract for goods and services received to date before requesting additional goods or services. Further, the reference guide is used only as supplemental information to the policy framework, which also does not contain such a requirement.

ID no.	Recommendation	Source report	Status per IRS	Status per GAO
11-05	Establish procedures to centrally review and monitor the timeliness of personnel action requests and approvals to help ensure compliance with the IRM and applicable Office of Personnel Management (OPM) regulations and guidance. (short-term)	Management Report: Improvements Are Needed to Enhance Internal Revenue Service's Internal Controls and Operating Effectiveness (GAO-11-494R, June 21, 2011), page 15.	Open. As of September 2011, IRS (1) issued clarifying guidance for personal action requests (PAR), (2) established a centralized quality review program to monitor the timeliness of PARs, and (3) developed new reports to assist in monitoring PAR timeliness. During fiscal year 2012, IRS will (1) finalize the Closeout Report that will assist in identifying pain points within the process to identify where to focus training and follow-up, (2) conduct training for HR specialists on the newly implemented standardized PAR process, and (3) issue communications to managers to ensure PARs are initiated timely.	Open. During our fiscal year 2011 audit, we continued to find instances in which the employee's request for personnel action was approved after the effective date of the action. While we verified that IRS established the Quality Assurance and Measures branch to help ensure compliance with the IRM and OPM regulations and guidance, IRS continues to implement new processes to improve the timeliness of personnel action requests and approvals. We will continue to assess IRS's actions during our fiscal year 2012 audit.
11-06	Adopt the local field office's timekeeping procedures or similar procedures for entering and verifying the accuracy of time and attendance information entered into the Single Entry Time Reporting System (SETR) throughout IRS for use by all units in which employees do not enter their own time charges directly to SETR. (short-term)	Management Report: Improvements Are Needed to Enhance Internal Revenue Service's Internal Controls and Operating Effectiveness (GAO-11-494R, June 21, 2011), page 17.	Closed. In August 2011, IRS modified Standard Operating Procedure (SOP) MPC-02, Time & Attendance Reporting, Approval and Maintenance Requirements, placed the revised SOP on the IRS internal web site, and forwarded it to all SETR Business Unit points of contact that are currently able to approve time sheets in SETR to disseminate.	Closed. The revised SOP states that business units may develop local office timekeeping procedures for entering and verifying the accuracy of time and attendance information entered into SETR if employees do not enter their own time; however, regardless of the specific procedures established, managers are now responsible for ensuring that the time entered in SETR for both weeks of the pay period for employees that do not enter their own time into SETR matches the source document prior to validating and electronically signing the employee's SETR timecard.

ID no.	Recommendation	Source report	Status per IRS	Status per GAO
11-07	Further revise the detailed procedures for implementing the requirement to validate the appropriateness of the National Finance Center (NFC) programming changes after such changes are made. These revisions should (1) clarify the criteria for determining which programming changes will be subject to validation, (2) identify officials responsible for making and documenting these determinations, and (3) require postimplementation statistical sampling from a targeted population that consists of employees who are most likely to be affected by the NFC programming changes. (short-term)	Management Report: Improvements Are Needed to Enhance Internal Revenue Service's Internal Controls and Operating Effectiveness (GAO-11-494R, June 21, 2011), page 20.	Closed. In November 2011, IRS updated and published the SOP on National Finance Center Change Requests. The SOP clarifies the criteria for determining which program changes will be subject to validation, identifies officials responsible for making and documenting these determinations, and outlines post-implementation testing that will be performed to validate the changes.	Closed. We reviewed IRS's revised SOP and verified that it clarifies the criteria for determining which program changes are subject to validation and identifies the officials responsible for making these determinations. Furthermore, the revised SOP establishes guidelines for postvalidation random sample testing from the population affected by the programming change.
11-08	Take steps to effectively implement procedures at the Beckley Finance Center requiring cash receipts to be immediately logged under dual control when first discovered in the mail room. (short-term)	Management Report: Improvements Are Needed to Enhance Internal Revenue Service's Internal Controls and Operating Effectiveness (GAO-11-494R, June 21, 2011), page 22.	Closed. In 2011, IRS conducted a review of the cash receipt deposit process using the process revised in August 2010 and determined that cash receipts were being logged under dual control. In addition, the contractor responsible for the mail room employees implemented a quality review process to ensure that those employees follow the revised check deposit process.	Closed. During our fiscal year 2011 audit, we verified that IRS effectively implemented procedures at the Beckley Finance Center requiring cash receipts to be immediately logged under dual control when first discovered in the mail room.
11-09	Take steps to effectively implement procedures at the Beckley Finance Center requiring mail room staff to maintain custody of the control log at all times. (short-term)	Management Report: Improvements Are Needed to Enhance Internal Revenue Service's Internal Controls and Operating Effectiveness (GAO-11-494R, June 21, 2011), page 22.	Closed. In 2011, IRS conducted a review of the cash receipt deposit process using the process revised in August 2010 and determined that the control log was properly maintained by mail room staff. In addition, the contractor responsible for the mail room employees implemented a quality review process to ensure that those employees follow the revised check deposit process.	Closed. During our fiscal year 2011 audit, we verified that IRS effectively implemented procedures at the Beckley Finance Center requiring mail room staff to maintain custody of the control log at all times.

ID no.	Recommendation	Source report	Status per IRS	Status per GAO
11-10	Take steps to effectively implement procedures at the Beckley Finance Center requiring the amount of cash receipts initially discovered in the mail room to be independently reconciled to the amount deposited and recorded in the general ledger. (short-term)	Management Report: Improvements Are Needed to Enhance Internal Revenue Service's Internal Controls and Operating Effectiveness (GAO-11-494R, June 21, 2011), page 22.	Closed. In 2011, IRS conducted a review of the cash receipt deposit process using the process revised in August 2010 and determined that cash receipts in the mail room were being independently reconciled to the amount deposited and recorded in the general ledger. In addition, the contractor responsible for the mail room employees implemented a quality review process to ensure that those employees follow the revised check deposit process.	Closed. During our fiscal year 2011 audit, we verified that IRS effectively implemented procedures at the Beckley Finance Center requiring the amount of cash receipts initially discovered in the mail room to be independently reconciled to the amount deposited and recorded in the general ledger.
11-11	Perform a review of all existing contracts under $100,000 that (1) do not have an appointed contracting officer's technical representative (COTR) and (2) do not require that contract employees obtain background investigations to assess whether the services performed under each contract warrant a requirement that contract employees obtain background investigations. (short-term)	Management Report: Improvements Are Needed to Enhance Internal Revenue Service's Internal Controls and Operating Effectiveness (GAO-11-494R, June 21, 2011), page 24.	Open. In December 2012, IRS will issue the Contractor Security Lifecycle Program Office policy specifying that IRS will review all existing service contracts under $100,000 by June 2013 and determine if they need to be modified to include additional background investigation requirements.	Open. IRS plans to determine whether the services performed under these contracts under review warrant obtaining background investigations on the contract employee(s) by June 2013 and will ensure all existing service contracts under $100,000 identified in the review contain the necessary security requirements by September 2013. Given the potential risk related to this recommendation, the estimated dates of IRS's corrective actions leave IRS exposed to a significant risk of allowing unauthorized access to IRS facilities or sensitive information, or both, for an extended period of time. We will continue to evaluate IRS's actions during our fiscal year 2012 audit.

ID no.	Recommendation	Source report	Status per IRS	Status per GAO
11-12	Based on a review of all existing contracts under $100,000 without an appointed contracting officer's technical representative (COTR) that should require contract employees to obtain favorable background investigation results, amend those contracts to require that favorable background investigations be obtained for all relevant contract employees before routine, unescorted, unsupervised physical access to taxpayer information is granted. (short-term)	Management Report: Improvements Are Needed to Enhance Internal Revenue Service's Internal Controls and Operating Effectiveness (GAO-11-494R, June 21, 2011), page 24.	Open. By September 2012, IRS will ensure all existing service contracts under $100,000, identified in the above-mentioned review, contain the necessary security requirements.	Open. IRS's efforts to address this recommendation are ongoing. IRS stated that by September 2012, it will ensure that all existing service contracts under $100,000 will contain the necessary security requirements. We will continue to evaluate IRS's actions during our fiscal year 2012 audit.

ID no.	Recommendation	Source report	Status per IRS	Status per GAO
11-13	Establish a policy requiring collaborative oversight between IRS's key offices in determining whether potential service contracts involve routine, unescorted, unsupervised physical access to taxpayer information, thus requiring background investigations, regardless of contract award amount. This policy should include a process for the requiring business unit to communicate to the Office of Procurement and the Human Capital Office the services to be provided under the contract and any potential exposure of taxpayer information to contract employees providing the services, and for all three units to (1) evaluate the risk of exposure of taxpayer information prior to finalizing and awarding the contract and (2) ensure that the final contract requires favorable background investigations as applicable, commensurate with the assessed risk. (short-term)	Management Report: Improvements Are Needed to Enhance Internal Revenue Service's Internal Controls and Operating Effectiveness (GAO-11-494R, June 21, 2011), page 24.	Open. By December 2012, IRS will establish a policy and associated procedures requiring business units to (1) identify service contracts where contractors will have routine, unescorted, unsupervised, physical access to taxpayer information; (2) document the risk of exposure to taxpayer data; and (3) ensure that the requirements of the Internal Revenue Service Acquisition Procedures 1052.204-9005, Submission of Security Forms and Related Materials, are included in the contract, as applicable.	Open. IRS's efforts to address our recommendation are ongoing. We will continue to evaluate IRS's actions during our fiscal year 2012 audit.

ID no.	Recommendation	Source report	Status per IRS	Status per GAO
11-14	Establish procedures to provide a consistent methodology for calculating and establishing allowable deposit courier trip time limits to be used by both service center campuses (SCC) and lockbox banks that would assist in detecting potential unauthorized stops or other contractual violations by deposit couriers. Such procedures should include instructions for documenting and supporting how the trip limits were determined and require justification and approval for all established time limits that exceed the average trip time. (short-term)	Management Report: Improvements Are Needed to Enhance Internal Revenue Service's Internal Controls and Operating Effectiveness (GAO-11-494R, June 21, 2011), page 27.	Closed. In April 2011, IRS updated the SOWs for all of its SP sites to reflect new delivery timeframes for daily deposits to the financial institution drop-off location based on data gathered during courier surveillance. In January 2011, IRS updated the Lockbox Security Guidelines (LSG) 2.16, Establishing Courier Timeframes, which serves as the SOW for Lockbox banks, to include procedures to provide a consistent methodology to calculate and establish allowable time limits for courier deliveries to Lockbox banks. The LSG procedures document and support how the trip limits are determined and require justification and approval for deviations from established time limits. IRS and FMS program offices completed their review of alternative solutions to mitigate deposit courier travel time deficiencies in December 2011. Based on this, Real-Time Global Positioning System technology will be installed on all lockbox deposit courier service vehicles starting in March 2012.	Open. The procedures that IRS established in this area during fiscal year 2011 would not have been effective in detecting potential unauthorized stops or other contractual violations by deposit couriers. For example, the documented allowable time limit at one of the lockbox banks we visited was 22 minutes; however, bank policy allowed for an additional 15 minutes beyond the documented time limit before couriers were asked to provide an explanation for the delay. At another lockbox bank we visited, we found that the bank allowed 36 minutes for deposit trips before the couriers were questioned. Based on a 3-month analysis performed by the bank, the average deposit trip time was 21 minutes. It is unclear why the bank allowed for an additional 15 minutes (over 70 percent of the average time) before deposit couriers are questioned. We will continue to evaluate IRS's corrective actions, including use of Real-Time Global Positioning System Technology on courier vehicles, during our fiscal year 2012 audit.
11-15	Establish procedures to require periodic reassessments of and updates to deposit courier allowable trip time limits to account for changes in courier routes or other conditions that may affect trip times. (short-term)	Management Report: Improvements Are Needed to Enhance Internal Revenue Service's Internal Controls and Operating Effectiveness (GAO-11-494R, June 21, 2011), page 27.	Closed. In April 2011, IRS updated the IRM section on the Manual Deposit Process to reflect established timeframes that will be re-evaluated each year during the annual unannounced security reviews or whenever changes occur in the drop-off location. In November 2011, IRS updated this IRM section to establish procedures that require periodic reassessments of, and updates to, deposit courier allowable trip limits to account for changes in courier routes or other conditions that may affect trip times.	Closed. In response to our recommendation, IRS took action to update IRM 3.8.45 Manual Deposit Process, to include procedures to reassess SCC deposit courier trip times during unannounced security reviews or whenever there is a change in depository location. In addition, IRS updated the LSG to require that lockbox banks perform an annual detailed analysis to establish acceptable courier time frames.

ID no.	Recommendation	Source report	Status per IRS	Status per GAO
11-16	Enforce existing contractual requirements for the cargo doors of contract courier vehicles to be locked after picking up taxpayer information. (short-term)	Management Report: Improvements Are Needed to Enhance Internal Revenue Service's Internal Controls and Operating Effectiveness (GAO-11-494R, June 21, 2011), page 29.	Closed. IRS strengthened its enforcement by conducting monthly random reviews of contractor adherence to the secure transport requirements, including the requirement for cargo doors of contract courier vehicles to be locked after picking up taxpayer information. To date, the monthly random reviews indicate that the contractor is complying with the requirements to lock the vehicle cargo doors after picking up taxpayer information. The contractors have been in compliance with secure transport requirements since April 2011. In addition, the contractor implemented its own internal review process and reports the results to the Contracting Officer's Technical Representative (COTR).	Open. During our March 2012 internal control testing at an SCC, we found that IRS did not apply these procedures to instances where contract couriers were transporting items including taxpayer information to multiple IRS locations. We will evaluate the effectiveness of IRS's enforcement actions in this area during our fiscal year 2012 audit fieldwork.

ID no.	Recommendation	Source report	Status per IRS	Status per GAO
11-17	Establish procedures to prevent or detect unauthorized access to taxpayer information in contract courier vehicles during transit. These procedures should detail specific activities to be performed by both the business unit sending and receiving the information transported by the contract courier. (short-term)	Management Report: Improvements Are Needed to Enhance Internal Revenue Service's Internal Controls and Operating Effectiveness (GAO-11-494R, June 21, 2011), page 29.	Closed. In December 2011, IRS established procedures in IRM 3.13.62, Campus Document Services—Media Transport and Control, to prevent and detect unauthorized access to taxpayer information in contract courier vehicles during transit to and from offsite processing facilities. The IRM directs Submission Processing (SP) personnel to ensure the transportation truck is secured when it leaves the site with taxpayer material. When the material is delivered to the SP site, SP personnel will ensure the truck is still secured and will immediately report any discrepancies. The IRM also states that a random monthly managerial review must be conducted and documented with actions taken to alert headquarters to any issues. In addition, IRS continues its monthly random review of contractor adherence to the secure transport requirements started in April 2011. To date, the monthly random reviews confirm that the contractor is complying with the requirement to lock the vehicle cargo doors after picking up taxpayer information.	Open. While IRS established procedures to help prevent and detect unauthorized access to taxpayer information in contract courier vehicles, these procedures are currently only directed at the Wage and Investment (W&I) business unit. We were unable to identify similar procedures directed at the other IRS business units that may also transport taxpayer information from one IRS location to another, including Large Business and International (LB&I), Small Business/Self Employed (SB/SE), and Tax Exempt/Government Entities (TE/GE). We will continue to evaluate IRS's actions during our fiscal year 2012 audit.

ID no.	Recommendation	Source report	Status per IRS	Status per GAO
11-18	Revise the guidance for conducting the periodic reviews of the contract couriers transporting taxpayer information from one IRS processing facility to another to include procedures for (1) physically verifying that courier vehicle cargo doors are locked after picking up this information and remain locked during transit to the final destination and (2) documenting the basis for the reviewer's conclusions. (short-term)	Management Report: Improvements Are Needed to Enhance Internal Revenue Service's Internal Controls and Operating Effectiveness (GAO-11-494R, June 21, 2011), page 29.	Closed. In December 2011, IRS revised the guidance for conducting periodic reviews of the contract couriers transporting taxpayer information to include physically verifying that courier vehicle cargo doors are locked after pick-up and remain locked during transit to the final destination. IRM 3.16.62, Campus Document Services—Media Transport and Control, directs Submission Processing (SP) personnel to ensure the transportation truck is secured when it leaves the site with taxpayer material. When the material is delivered to the SP site, SP personnel will ensure the truck is still secured and will immediately report any discrepancies. The IRM also states that a random monthly managerial review of the process must be conducted and documented with actions taken to alert headquarters to any issues. Starting in January 2012, Submission Processing will conduct monthly reviews and document the results. In October 2011, IRS revised the Logistics Services contract sub-COTR desk guide to include guidance for conducting the periodic reviews of the contract couriers transporting taxpayer information from one IRS processing facility to another. The guidance outlines the procedures for physically verifying and documenting that courier vehicle cargo doors are locked. In addition, IRS continues its monthly random review of contractor adherence to the secure transport requirements started in April 2011. To date, the monthly random reviews confirm that the contractor is complying with the requirement to lock the vehicle cargo doors after picking up taxpayer information.	Open. We found that IRS's revised guidance for conducting periodic reviews of the contract couriers transporting taxpayer information does not include the use of contract couriers transporting taxpayer information to non-Wage and Investment (W&I) business units, nor does it take into account instances where contract couriers are making multiple stops to various business units. We will continue to evaluate IRS's efforts during our fiscal year 2012 audit.

ID no.	Recommendation	Source report	Status per IRS	Status per GAO
11-19	Revise the IRM to include a comprehensive process that Small Business / Self-Employed (SBSE) unit managers should follow when performing reviews of the document transmittal process for determining whether staff are (1) maintaining control copies of document transmittal forms, (2) reconciling all document transmittal forms on a biweekly basis to ensure that all transmittals were received, and (3) following up on transmittals that are not timely acknowledged. (short-term)	Management Report: Improvements Are Needed to Enhance Internal Revenue Service's Internal Controls and Operating Effectiveness (GAO-11-494R, June 21, 2011), page 31.	Closed. In December 2011, IRS published an update to IRM 1.4.50, Collection Group Manager, Territory Manager and Area Director Operational Aid. The update clarified the actions management should take to determine whether staff are (1) maintaining control copies of document transmittal forms, (2) reconciling all document transmittal forms on a bi-weekly basis to ensure that all transmittals are acknowledged, and (3) performing the follow-up procedures required in IRM 5.1.2.4.4(1)9, Collection Field Clerical Staff Procedures for Form 795/795A Processing.	Closed. In response to our recommendation, in December 2011, IRS published the update to IRM 1.4.50-Collection Group Manager, Territory Manager and Area Director Operational Aid. This revision includes provisions that management should take to determine whether their staff are: (1) maintaining control copies of document transmittal forms, (2) reconciling all document transmittal forms on a biweekly basis to ensure that all transmittals were received, and (3) following up on transmittals that are not timely acknowledged.
11-20	Revise the IRM to include specifying minimally acceptable steps the Small Business/Self-Employed (SB/SE) unit managers should follow in documenting the results of required reviews of the document transmittal process. (short-term)	Management Report: Improvements Are Needed to Enhance Internal Revenue Service's Internal Controls and Operating Effectiveness (GAO-11-494R, June 22, 2011), page 31.	Closed. In December 2011, IRS published the update to IRM 1.4.50, Collection Group Manager, Territory Manager and Area Director Operational Aid. The update clarified the minimally acceptable documentation that SB/SE managers should complete when conducting the reviews and reporting the results.	Closed. In response to our recommendation, IRS updated IRM 1.4.50, Collection Group Manager, Territory Manager, and Area Manager Director Operational Aid, in December 2011. This includes minimum steps for SBSE unit managers to follow in their reviews of the document transmittal process.
11-21	Define and specify in the IRM which types of IRS facilities constitute a processing facility. (short-term)	Management Report: Improvements Are Needed to Enhance Internal Revenue Service's Internal Controls and Operating Effectiveness (GAO-11-494R, June 21, 2011), page 33.	Closed. In October 2011, IRS updated and published IRM 10.2.2, Physical Security Compliance Reviews, to require recurring compliance reviews every 2 years at off-site campus locations that perform Receipt and Control or Submission Processing activities. As a result, off-site campus locations now undergo compliance reviews at the same frequency as processing and computing center facilities.	Closed. We verified that the IRM was updated to reflect the inclusion of off-site campus locations with Receipt and Control and submission processing type functions under the 2-year compliance review requirement.

ID no.	Recommendation	Source report	Status per IRS	Status per GAO
11-22	Perform an assessment of off-site processing facilities to determine the frequency with which compliance reviews should be performed for these locations commensurate with the specific operational activities performed and the assessed level of risk associated with the facility. (short-term)	Management Report: Improvements Are Needed to Enhance Internal Revenue Service's Internal Controls and Operating Effectiveness (GAO-11-494R, June 21, 2011), page 34.	Closed. In October 2011, after performing an assessment of the off-site processing facilities, IRS updated and published IRM 10.2.2, Physical Security Compliance Reviews, that requires recurring compliance reviews every 2 years at off-site processing facilities.	Closed. IRS performed an assessment of the off-site processing facilities. As a result of that assessment and our recommendation, IRS determined that compliance reviews for off-site campus locations with Receipt and Control and submission processing type functions should be performed on a recurring basis every 2 years, which is the same frequency as processing and computing center facilities.
11-23	Based on the results of an assessment of off-site processing facilities that process taxpayer receipts and related taxpayer information, revise the IRM to specify the frequency with which compliance reviews should be performed at these facilities. (short-term)	Management Report: Improvements Are Needed to Enhance Internal Revenue Service's Internal Controls and Operating Effectiveness (GAO-11-494R, June 21, 2011), page 34.	Closed. In October 2011, IRS updated and published IRM 10.2.2, Physical Security Compliance Reviews, that requires recurring compliance reviews every 2 years at off-site processing facilities.	Closed. IRS performed an assessment of the off-site processing facilities. As a result of that assessment and our recommendation, IRS updated IRM 10.2.2 to require recurring compliance reviews every 2 years for off-site campus locations with Receipt and Control and submission processing type functions.
11-24	Revise the post orders for the service center campuses (SCC) and lockbox bank security guards to include specific procedures for timely reporting exterior lighting outages to SCC or lockbox bank facilities management. These procedures should specify (1) whom to contact to report lighting outages and (2) how to document and track lighting outages until resolved. (short-term)	Management Report: Improvements Are Needed to Enhance Internal Revenue Service's Internal Controls and Operating Effectiveness (GAO-11-494R, June 21, 2011), page 35.	Open. In November 2011, IRS updated IRM 10.2.12, Security Guard and Explosive Detector Dog Services and Programs, to include the requirements for reporting lighting outages and specify (1) whom to contact to report lighting outages and (2) how to document and track lighting outages until resolved. In fiscal year 2012, IRS will update the IRM to require after-dark reviews in the lockbox security guards' post orders, and will update LSG section 2.3.4.1 (6) (c) and 2.3.4.1.3, and Exhibit 13 of LSG 2.3, for consistency.	Open. IRS's efforts to address our recommendation are ongoing. We will continue to evaluate IRS's actions during our fiscal year 2012 audit.

ID no.	Recommendation	Source report	Status per IRS	Status per GAO
11-25	Revise the nature and scope of the service center campuses' (SCC) and lockbox banks' physical security reviews to include periodic after dark assessments of physical security controls. (short-term)	Management Report: Improvements Are Needed to Enhance Internal Revenue Service's Internal Controls and Operating Effectiveness (GAO-11-494R, June 21, 2011), page 35.	Closed. In November 2011, the IRS updated IRM 10.2.12, Security Guard and Explosive Detector Dog Services and Programs, to require that physical security reviews of the Service Center Campuses include periodic, after-dark assessments of physical security. In January 2012, the IRS updated the Lockbox Security Guidelines, Post Orders, and Patrol and Event/Incident Reporting to include requirements for the guards to conduct patrols of the exterior of the lockbox site to include periodic after-dark physical security assessments and to report lighting outages with specific procedures for timely reporting of exterior lighting outages to the Lockbox facilities management.	Open. While IRS included requirements in the post orders for security guards to report lighting outages for repair, it has not included requirements for periodic after-dark assessments of physical security controls, or verification that guards are properly reporting light outages in the routine SCC physical security reviews. We will continue to evaluate IRS's actions during our fiscal year 2012 audit.
11-26	Take steps to effectively implement the procedures requiring property staff to verify that the asset purchase price shown in the Asset Management Report agrees with the asset purchase price shown in the Integrated Financial System (IFS) and to resolve any variances before entering the information into the Information Technology Asset Management System (ITAMS). (short-term)	Management Report: Improvements Are Needed to Enhance Internal Revenue Service's Internal Controls and Operating Effectiveness (GAO-11-494R, June 21. 2011), page 37.	Closed. In February 2011, IRS revised its internal standard operating procedures to require that Asset Management personnel conduct appropriate research to validate the price data supplied on the Asset Management Report (ARM) against the pricing information in webRTS, prior to uploading the data in ITAMS.	Open. IRS revised its operating procedures to require that property staff conduct research to ensure that the price of an asset on the ARM report agrees with the price listed in IFS. In addition, IRS is required to research and resolve any variances before uploading an asset in ITAMS. IRS has replaced ITAMS with Knowledge Incident/Problem Service Asset Management (KISAM); however, similar to ITAMS, KISAM is not integrated with IFS. We will evaluate the effectiveness of IRS's actions and the new inventory system during our fiscal year 2012 audit.
11-27	Finalize procedures requiring that copier hard drives be removed and destroyed or otherwise appropriately cleaned before disposing of copiers. (short-term)	Management Report: Improvements Are Needed to Enhance Internal Revenue Service's Internal Controls and Operating Effectiveness (GAO-11-494R, June 21, 2011), page 39.	Closed. In March 2011, the National Copier Contract COTR published written procedures to the REFM field offices requiring that copier hard drives be removed and destroyed prior to disposing of copiers.	Closed. During our fiscal year 2011 audit, IRS finalized procedures requiring that copier hard drives be removed and destroyed or properly cleaned prior to disposal.

ID no.	Recommendation	Source report	Status per IRS	Status per GAO
11-28	Revise the IRM to incorporate the new copier disposal procedures that require that copier hard drives be removed and destroyed or otherwise appropriately cleaned before disposing of copiers. (short-term)	Management Report: Improvements Are Needed to Enhance Internal Revenue Service's Internal Controls and Operating Effectiveness (GAO-11-494R, June 21, 2011), page 39.	Closed. IRS revised two IRM sections in 2011 to include the proper handling procedures of copier hard drives prior to copier disposal.	Closed. During our fiscal year 2011 audit, IRS revised its IRM to incorporate the new copier disposal procedures. The IRM now includes guidance for removing and destroying or otherwise appropriately cleaning copier hard drives before disposing of copiers.
11-29	Issue a memorandum to all business units reminding them that only designated Real Estate Facilities Management (REFM) staff are authorized to dispose of copiers. (short-term)	Management Report: Improvements Are Needed to Enhance Internal Revenue Service's Internal Controls and Operating Effectiveness (GAO-11-494R, June 21, 2011), page 39.	Closed. In July 2011, the Director, REFM, issued a memorandum to all business units reminding them that only designated REFM staff are authorized to dispose of copiers. This information was also referenced in the updates to the IRM.	Closed. During our fiscal year 2011 audit, IRS issued a memorandum to all business units. The memorandum reminds business units that the disposal of copiers must be coordinated through REFM.
12-01	Establish and document an inventory of the specific systems involved in IRS's financial reporting process, including (1) describing what role each system plays in the financial reporting process, (2) concluding whether each system is considered to be material to financial reporting and why, and (3) denoting whether each system is controlled by IRS or by an external service provider and, if the latter, identifying the service provider. (short-term)	Management Report: Improvements Are Needed to Enhance Internal Revenue Service's Internal Controls and Operating Effectiveness (GAO-12-683R, June 25, 2012), page 13.	Because this is a new recommendation, GAO did not obtain information on IRS's status in addressing it.	Open. This is a recent recommendation. We will verify IRS's corrective actions during our fiscal year 2012 and future audits.

ID no.	Recommendation	Source report	Status per IRS	Status per GAO
12-02	Enhance existing policies and procedures pertaining to monitoring internal control over the automated systems operated by IRS personnel to specifically provide for routine, documented monitoring of the specific internal controls within its financial reporting systems that are intended to ensure the integrity of the data reported in the financial statements and other financial reports. This monitoring process should (1) involve both automated systems specialists and individuals with expertise in accounting and reporting, as appropriate, (2) encompass the specific automated internal controls that affect the authorizing, processing, transmitting, or reporting of material financial transactions, and (3) be designed to determine whether these internal controls are in place and operating effectively. (short-term)	Management Report: Improvements Are Needed to Enhance Internal Revenue Service's Internal Controls and Operating Effectiveness (GAO-12-683R, June 25, 2012), page 13.	Because this is a new recommendation, GAO did not obtain information on IRS's status in addressing it.	Open. This is a recent recommendation. We will verify IRS's corrective actions during our fiscal year 2012 and future audits.

ID no.	Recommendation	Source report	Status per IRS	Status per GAO
12-03	For any system identified as material to IRS's financial reporting process which is controlled by an external service provider, establish policies and procedures requiring and defining a routine, documented process for coordinating with the service provider to appropriately monitor related internal control. This may entail establishing an agreement with each service provider to allow IRS personnel access to either (1) the system concerned, as necessary to perform appropriate monitoring of internal control over financial reporting or (2) periodic reports prepared in accordance with Statements on Standards for Attestation Engagements (SSAE) No. 16 documenting the results of monitoring performed by the service provider. (short-term)	Management Report: Improvements Are Needed to Enhance Internal Revenue Service's Internal Controls and Operating Effectiveness (GAO-12-683R, June 25, 2012), page 13.	Because this is a new recommendation, GAO did not obtain information on IRS's status in addressing it.	Open. This is a recent recommendation. We will verify IRS's corrective actions during our fiscal year 2012 and future audits.

ID no.	Recommendation	Source report	Status per IRS	Status per GAO
12-04	Establish policies and procedures with respect to any external financial reporting system IRS personnel themselves do not directly monitor that specify required steps to routinely review periodic reports prepared by service providers' auditors in accordance with SSAE No. 16, including steps to document (1) an assessment of whether a review's scope, methodology, and timing is appropriate to satisfy IRS's objectives; (2) any control deficiencies disclosed in the report, and an assessment of their materiality to IRS's financial reporting process and related risks; and (3) any compensating internal controls needed to mitigate any actual or potential effects of identified deficiencies upon IRS's internal and external financial reports resulting from any (a) material weakness, or (b) significant shortcoming in the scope, methodology, or timing of any SSAE No. 16 report reviewed relative to IRS's internal control objectives. (short-term)	Management Report: Improvements Are Needed to Enhance Internal Revenue Service's Internal Controls and Operating Effectiveness (GAO-12-683R, June 25, 2012), page 13.	Because this is a new recommendation, GAO did not obtain information on IRS's status in addressing it.	Open. This is a recent recommendation. We will verify IRS's corrective actions during our fiscal year 2012 and future audits.

ID no.	Recommendation	Source report	Status per IRS	Status per GAO
12-05	Update IRS's procedures for comparing tax revenue recorded in the general ledger to detailed tax revenue transactions recorded in the master files to (1) establish minimum criteria defining a significant or unusual variance and (2) specify the steps required to effectively evaluate and resolve these variances. (short-term)	Management Report: Improvements Are Needed to Enhance Internal Revenue Service's Internal Controls and Operating Effectiveness (GAO-12-683R, June 25, 2012), page 16.	Because this is a new recommendation, GAO did not obtain information on IRS's status in addressing it.	Open. This is a recent recommendation. We will verify IRS's corrective actions during our fiscal year 2012 and future audits.
12-06	Update IRS's procedures for comparing tax revenue recorded in the general ledger to detailed tax revenue transactions recorded in the master files to require that management reviews ensure preparers evaluate and resolve unusual or significant variances. (short-term)	Management Report: Improvements Are Needed to Enhance Internal Revenue Service's Internal Controls and Operating Effectiveness (GAO-12-683R, June 25, 2012), page 16.	Because this is a new recommendation, GAO did not obtain information on IRS's status in addressing it.	Open. This is a recent recommendation. We will verify IRS's corrective actions during our fiscal year 2012 and future audits.
12-07	Establish and document procedures for ensuring that recorded reimbursable revenue, transfers in without reimbursement, and accounts receivable from the Department of the Treasury Forfeiture Fund (TFF) conform to federal accounting standards. (short-term)	Management Report: Improvements Are Needed to Enhance Internal Revenue Service's Internal Controls and Operating Effectiveness (GAO-12-683R, June 25, 2012), page 18.	Because this is a new recommendation, GAO did not obtain information on IRS's status in addressing it.	Open. This is a recent recommendation. We will verify IRS's corrective actions during our fiscal year 2012 and future audits.
12-08	Establish requirements specifying a required time frame for territory managers to perform the required review and approval of completed audit management checklists. (short-term)	Management Report: Improvements Are Needed to Enhance Internal Revenue Service's Internal Controls and Operating Effectiveness (GAO-12-683R, June 25, 2012), page 20.	Because this is a new recommendation, GAO did not obtain information on IRS's status in addressing it.	Open. This is a recent recommendation. We will verify IRS's corrective actions during our fiscal year 2012 and future audits.

ID no.	Recommendation	Source report	Status per IRS	Status per GAO
12-09	Establish procedures requiring Physical Security and Emergency Preparedness (PSEP) headquarters to centrally monitor compliance with the audit management checklist process to ensure that (1) PSEP analysts timely complete their physical security reviews using the proper audit management checklists and (2) territory managers timely review and properly document their reviews of completed audit management checklists. (short-term)	Management Report: Improvements Are Needed to Enhance Internal Revenue Service's Internal Controls and Operating Effectiveness (GAO-12-683R, June 25, 2012), page 20.	Because this is a new recommendation, GAO did not obtain information on IRS's status in addressing it.	Open. This is a recent recommendation. We will verify IRS's corrective actions during our fiscal year 2012 and future audits.
12-10	Update the IRM to specify steps to be followed to prevent campus support clerks as well as any other employees who process payments through the electronic check presentment system from making adjustments to taxpayer accounts. (short-term)	Management Report: Improvements Are Needed to Enhance Internal Revenue Service's Internal Controls and Operating Effectiveness (GAO-12-683R, June 25, 2012), page 22.	Because this is a new recommendation, GAO did not obtain information on IRS's status in addressing it.	Open. This is a recent recommendation. We will verify IRS's corrective actions during our fiscal year 2012 and future audits.
12-11	Implement the September 2011 revised policy that requires an independent review of the rent check summary report to help ensure that the monthly rent allocation process is properly completed. (short-term)	Management Report: Improvements Are Needed to Enhance Internal Revenue Service's Internal Controls and Operating Effectiveness (GAO-12-683R, June 25, 2012), page 25.	Because this is a new recommendation, GAO did not obtain information on IRS's status in addressing it.	Open. This is a recent recommendation. We will verify IRS's corrective actions during our fiscal year 2012 and future audits.
12-12	Establish a policy requiring an independent review of changes made by the rent processing administrator to non-GSA lease data in the Graphic Database Interface system (GDI). (short-term)	Management Report: Improvements Are Needed to Enhance Internal Revenue Service's Internal Controls and Operating Effectiveness (GAO-12-683R, June 25, 2012), page 25.	Because this is a new recommendation, GAO did not obtain information on IRS's status in addressing it.	Open. This is a recent recommendation. We will verify IRS's corrective actions during our fiscal year 2012 and future audits.

ID no.	Recommendation	Source report	Status per IRS	Status per GAO
12-13	Revise existing written procedures to require supervisory review of the Computer-Aided Facilities Management (CAFM) Quarterly Review Certifications and Statistics against the Graphic Database Interface system (GDI) validation walkthrough sheets. (short-term)	Management Report: Improvements Are Needed to Enhance Internal Revenue Service's Internal Controls and Operating Effectiveness (GAO-12-683R, June 25, 2012), page 27.	Because this is a new recommendation, GAO did not obtain information on IRS's status in addressing it.	Open. This is a recent recommendation. We will verify IRS's corrective actions during our fiscal year 2012 and future audits.
12-14	Establish mechanisms to monitor the implementation of and compliance with the revised policy established in October 2011 that requires field CAFM program managers to maintain GDI Quarterly Review documentation, including GDI validation walkthrough sheets and GDI Quarterly Review certifications. (short-term)	Management Report: Improvements Are Needed to Enhance Internal Revenue Service's Internal Controls and Operating Effectiveness (GAO-12-683R, June 25, 2012), page 28.	Because this is a new recommendation, GAO did not obtain information on IRS's status in addressing it.	Open. This is a recent recommendation. We will verify IRS's corrective actions during our fiscal year 2012 and future audits.
12-15	Establish mechanisms to monitor the implementation of and compliance with the revised policy established in October 2011 that defines the type of errors that should be captured on the CAFM Quarterly Review Certifications to help ensure that field CAFM program managers consistently compile the errors found in their quarterly reviews for compilation in the overall CAFM Quarterly Review Statistics. (short-term)	Management Report: Improvements Are Needed to Enhance Internal Revenue Service's Internal Controls and Operating Effectiveness (GAO-12-683R, June 25, 2012), page 28.	Because this is a new recommendation, GAO did not obtain information on IRS's status in addressing it.	Open. This is a recent recommendation. We will verify IRS's corrective actions during our fiscal year 2012 and future audits.

GAO-12-695 Status of Recommendations

ID no.	Recommendation	Source report	Status per IRS	Status per GAO
12-16	Establish procedures to require the Office of Financial Reporting to ensure that extracted Graphic Database Interface system (GDI) data used to calculate the leasehold improvement disposal estimate is complete and accurate. (short-term)	Management Report: Improvements Are Needed to Enhance Internal Revenue Service's Internal Controls and Operating Effectiveness (GAO-12-683R, June 25, 2012), page 31.	Because this is a new recommendation, GAO did not obtain information on IRS's status in addressing it.	Open. This is a recent recommendation. We will verify IRS's corrective actions during our fiscal year 2012 and future audits.
12-17	Implement the revised January 2012 procedures requiring comparison of the leases used in the prior year with the current year leases to help ensure that expired leases have not been extended and thus, are only counted once in the disposal estimates. (short-term)	Management Report: Improvements Are Needed to Enhance Internal Revenue Service's Internal Controls and Operating Effectiveness (GAO-12-683R, June 25, 2012), page 31.	Because this is a new recommendation, GAO did not obtain information on IRS's status in addressing it.	Open. This is a recent recommendation. We will verify IRS's corrective actions during our fiscal year 2012 and future audits.
12-18	Implement the revised January 2012 procedures requiring preparation and review of leasehold improvement disposal calculations quarterly. (short-term)	Management Report: Improvements Are Needed to Enhance Internal Revenue Service's Internal Controls and Operating Effectiveness (GAO-12-683R, June 25, 2012), page 31.	Because this is a new recommendation, GAO did not obtain information on IRS's status in addressing it.	Open. This is a recent recommendation. We will verify IRS's corrective actions during our fiscal year 2012 and future audits.
12-19	Provide training to contracting officers and contracting officers' technical representatives (COTR) on their specific procedural requirements for obtaining and maintaining end user documentation of receipt and acceptance of the good or service prior to entering acknowledgment of receipt and acceptance in the procurement system. (short-term)	Management Report: Improvements Are Needed to Enhance Internal Revenue Service's Internal Controls and Operating Effectiveness (GAO-12-683R, June 25, 2012), page 33.	Because this is a new recommendation, GAO did not obtain information on IRS's status in addressing it.	Open. This is a recent recommendation. We will verify IRS's corrective actions during our fiscal year 2012 and future audits.

ID no.	Recommendation	Source report	Status per IRS	Status per GAO
12-20	Establish a mechanism to periodically monitor contracting officers and contracting officers' technical representatives (COTR) compliance with the requirement to obtain and document end user confirmation of receipt prior to entering receipt and acceptance into the procurement system. (short-term)	Management Report: Improvements Are Needed to Enhance Internal Revenue Service's Internal Controls and Operating Effectiveness (GAO-12-683R, June 25, 2012), page 33.	Because this is a new recommendation, GAO did not obtain information on IRS's status in addressing it.	Open. This is a recent recommendation. We will verify IRS's corrective actions during our fiscal year 2012 and future audits.
12-21	Establish a mechanism for monitoring compliance with the existing requirement for employees and timekeepers to charge labor time spent on the Patient Protection and Affordable Care Act (PPACA) projects to the PPACA accounting code, such as through issuing periodic alerts, providing training and guidance, and/or having managers perform periodic reviews of employee labor time charges. (short-term)	Management Report: Improvements Are Needed to Enhance Internal Revenue Service's Internal Controls and Operating Effectiveness (GAO-12-683R, June 25, 2012), page 36.	Because this is a new recommendation, GAO did not obtain information on IRS's status in addressing it.	Open. This is a recent recommendation. We will verify IRS's corrective actions during our fiscal year 2012 and future audits.
12-22	Design and implement procedures specifying the review steps required to identify and research all transactions identified with a PPACA internal order number in the agency's expense files to confirm that they are PPACA-related expenses and, if so, to ensure that they are charged to the PPACA appropriation where appropriate. (short-term)	Management Report: Improvements Are Needed to Enhance Internal Revenue Service's Internal Controls and Operating Effectiveness (GAO-12-683R, June 25, 2012), page 37.	Because this is a new recommendation, GAO did not obtain information on IRS's status in addressing it.	Open. This is a recent recommendation. We will verify IRS's corrective actions during our fiscal year 2012 and future audits.

ID no.	Recommendation	Source report	Status per IRS	Status per GAO
12-23	Revise the payroll standard operating procedures (SOP) to specify steps that the human resource specialists are required to follow to ensure that each electronic time card is signed by an authorized official before the timecard is transmitted to the National Finance Center for processing and payment. (short-term)	Management Report: Improvements Are Needed to Enhance Internal Revenue Service's Internal Controls and Operating Effectiveness (GAO-12-683R, June 25, 2012), page 39.	Because this is a new recommendation, GAO did not obtain information on IRS's status in addressing it.	Open. This is a recent recommendation. We will verify IRS's corrective actions during our fiscal year 2012 and future audits.
12-24	Revise the payroll standard operating procedures (SOP) to require that the designated proxy for a manager required to approve time cards be at an equivalent or higher level as the manager, consistent with the IRM. (short-term)	Management Report: Improvements Are Needed to Enhance Internal Revenue Service's Internal Controls and Operating Effectiveness (GAO-12-683R, June 25, 2012), page 40.	Because this is a new recommendation, GAO did not obtain information on IRS's status in addressing it.	Open. This is a recent recommendation. We will verify IRS's corrective actions during our fiscal year 2012 and future audits.
12-25	Incorporate in the planned 2012 policy change requiring the manager or designated proxy to sign the electronic time card before transmitting payroll records to the National Finance Center the requirement that the designated proxy be at an equivalent or higher level than the employee's manager. (short-term)	Management Report: Improvements Are Needed to Enhance Internal Revenue Service's Internal Controls and Operating Effectiveness (GAO-12-683R, June 25, 2012), page 40.	Because this is a new recommendation, GAO did not obtain information on IRS's status in addressing it.	Open. This is a recent recommendation. We will verify IRS's corrective actions during our fiscal year 2012 and future audits.
12-26	Implement an edit control in IRS's time card system to identify and prevent the processing of time cards that have not been electronically signed. (short-term)	Management Report: Improvements Are Needed to Enhance Internal Revenue Service's Internal Controls and Operating Effectiveness (GAO-12-683R, June 25, 2012), page 40.	Because this is a new recommendation, GAO did not obtain information on IRS's status in addressing it.	Open. This is a recent recommendation. We will verify IRS's corrective actions during our fiscal year 2012 and future audits.

ID no.	Recommendation	Source report	Status per IRS	Status per GAO
12-27	Remind managers of their responsibilities, procedures, and required time frames for either granting or denying a within-grade pay increase for employees with below fully successful ratings, such as by providing alerts in HR Connect when a manager enters a less than fully successful rating or providing training to remind them of their responsibilities. (short-term)	Management Report: Improvements Are Needed to Enhance Internal Revenue Service's Internal Controls and Operating Effectiveness (GAO-12-683R, June 25, 2012), page 44.	Because this is a new recommendation, GAO did not obtain information on IRS's status in addressing it.	Open. This is a recent recommendation. We will verify IRS's corrective actions during our fiscal year 2012 and future audits.
12-28	Establish procedures for human resource specialists to track and monitor supervisory actions taken for employees with less than fully successful ratings that have a within-grade pay increase due date within 90 days to include specific required steps for following-up with managers to ensure the managers properly issue the employees a 60-day notification letter providing them an opportunity to improve their performance, make a timely determination on releasing or denying a within-grade pay increase, and properly carry out the requirements necessary to support the decision made. (short-term)	Management Report: Improvements Are Needed to Enhance Internal Revenue Service's Internal Controls and Operating Effectiveness (GAO-12-683R, June 25, 2012), page 44.	Because this is a new recommendation, GAO did not obtain information on IRS's status in addressing it.	Open. This is a recent recommendation. We will verify IRS's corrective actions during our fiscal year 2012 and future audits.

ID no.	Recommendation	Source report	Status per IRS	Status per GAO
12-29	Establish procedures for HR specialists to track and monitor supervisory actions taken for employees with less than fully successful ratings that have a within-grade pay increase due date within 90 days to include specific required steps for timely granting a within-grade pay increase to such employees who were not given a 60-day notification letter. (short-term)	Management Report: Improvements Are Needed to Enhance Internal Revenue Service's Internal Controls and Operating Effectiveness (GAO-12-683R, June 25, 2012), page 44.	Because this is a new recommendation, GAO did not obtain information on IRS's status in addressing it.	Open. This is a recent recommendation. We will verify IRS's corrective actions during our fiscal year 2012 and future audits.
12-30	Establish and document procedures for payroll staff to research and correct recycled errors from payroll processing on a regular and timely basis. (short-term)	Management Report: Improvements Are Needed to Enhance Internal Revenue Service's Internal Controls and Operating Effectiveness (GAO-12-683R, June 25, 2012), page 45.	Because this is a new recommendation, GAO did not obtain information on IRS's status in addressing it.	Open. This is a recent recommendation. We will verify IRS's corrective actions during our fiscal year 2012 and future audits.

Source: GAO and RS.

Appendix II: Open Recommendations Arranged by Material Weakness, Significant Deficiency, Compliance, or Other Control Deficiencies

For several years, we have reported material weaknesses, significant deficiencies, noncompliance with laws and regulations, and other control deficiencies in our annual financial statement audits and related management reports.[1] Appendix II provides summary information regarding the primary issue to which each open recommendation is most closely related. To compile this summary, we analyzed the nature of the open recommendations to relate them to the material weaknesses, significant deficiency, compliance issue, or other control deficiencies (not associated with a material weakness, significant deficiency, or compliance issue) identified as part of our financial statement audit.

Material Weakness: Unpaid Assessments

The Internal Revenue Service (IRS) has a material weakness in its internal control over the management of unpaid assessments resulting from the agency's (1) inability to rely on its general ledger for tax transactions and underlying subsidiary records to report federal taxes receivable, compliance assessments, and writeoffs in accordance with federal accounting standards without significant compensating procedures, (2) lack of transaction traceability for the reported balance in taxes receivable that comprises over 80 percent of IRS's total assets as of September 30, 2011, and an effective transaction-based subledger for unpaid tax assessment transactions, and (3) inability to effectively prevent or timely detect and correct errors in taxpayer accounts. The recommendations in table 12 address our related findings.

Table 12: Material Weakness: Controls over Unpaid Assessments

ID no.	Recommendation	Control activity
99-01	Manually review and eliminate duplicate or other assessments that have already been paid off to assure that all accounts related to a single assessment are appropriately credited for payments received. (short-term)	Accurate and timely recording of transactions and events
08-06	In instances where computer programs that control penalty assessments are not functioning in accordance with the intent of the IRM, take appropriate action to correct the programs so that they function in accordance with the IRM. (long-term)	Accurate and timely recording of transactions and events

[1]See GAO, *Financial Audit: IRS's Fiscal Years 2011 and 2010 Financial Statements*, GAO-12-165 (Washington, D.C.: Nov. 10, 2011); and *Management Report: Improvements Are Needed to Further Enhance the Internal Revenue Service's Internal Controls and Operating Effectiveness*, GAO-12-683R (Washington, D.C.: June 25, 2012) for the fiscal year 2011 reports.

ID no.	Recommendation	Control activity
10-01	Review the results of IRS's unpaid assessments compensating statistical estimation process to identify and document instances where systemic limitations in the Custodial Detail Data Base (CDDB) resulted in misclassifications of account balances that, in turn, resulted in material inaccuracies in the amounts of reported unpaid tax assessments. (short-term)	Accurate and timely recording of transactions and events
10-02	Research and implement programming changes to allow the Custodial Detail Data Base (CDDB) to more accurately classify such accounts among the three categories of unpaid tax assessments. (short-term)	Accurate and timely recording of transactions and events
10-03	Research and identify control weaknesses resulting in inaccuracies or errors in taxpayer accounts that materially affect the financial reporting of unpaid tax assessments. (short-term)	Accurate and timely recording of transactions and events
10-04	Once IRS identifies the control weaknesses that result in inaccuracies or errors that materially affect the financial reporting of unpaid tax assessments, implement control procedures to routinely prevent, or to detect and correct, such errors. (short-term)	Accurate and timely recording of transactions and events

Source: GAO.

Material Weakness: Information Security

IRS has control deficiencies over information security that result primarily from IRS not having fully implemented key components of its information security program. These weaknesses, collectively, represent a material weakness. For example, (1) IRS's testing did not detect many of the vulnerabilities we identified and did not assess a key application in its current environment, and (2) IRS did not effectively validate corrective actions reported to resolve previously identified control deficiencies. Although IRS has made some progress in addressing previous control deficiencies we identified in its information systems and physical security controls, as of March 2012, there were 118 open recommendations designed to help IRS improve its information systems security controls. Those recommendations are reported separately and are not included in this report primarily because of the sensitive nature of some of the issues.[2]

---

[2]Although most of our recommendations regarding our information security work are sensitive and reported to IRS separately, we have reported our objectives, summary results, and nonsensitive recommendations in a publicly available report. See GAO, *Information Security: IRS Needs to Enhance Internal Control over Financial Reporting and Taxpayer Data*, GAO-12-393 (Washington, D.C.: Mar. 16, 2012).

Significant Deficiency: Tax Refund Disbursements

IRS has several control deficiencies over its tax refund disbursements. In our audit of IRS's fiscal year 2011 financial statements,[3] we reported a significant deficiency in IRS's internal control over tax refund disbursements that resulted from (1) IRS not having effectively addressed the deficiencies in internal control over manual tax refunds that we have reported in previous years,[4] (2) additional deficiencies in internal control over manual tax refunds we identified during our fiscal year 2011 audit, and (3) continued deficiencies in IRS's internal control over processing of claims for the First-time Homebuyer Credit (FTHBC). These control deficiencies related to the monitoring of manual refunds, training of staff having key roles in refund processing, and documentation of FTHBC claims. The recommendations in table 13 address our related findings.

Table 13: Significant Deficiency: Tax Refund Disbursements

ID no.	Recommendation	Control activity
05-38	Enforce requirements for monitoring accounts and reviewing monitoring of accounts for manual refunds. (short-term)	Reviews by management at the functional or activity level
05-39	Enforce requirements for documenting monitoring actions and supervisory review for manual refunds. (short-term)	Appropriate documentation of transactions and internal controls
07-08	Require that managers or supervisors provide the manual refund initiators in their units with training on the most current requirements to help ensure that they fulfill their responsibilities to monitor manual refunds and document their monitoring actions to prevent the issuance of duplicate refunds. (short-term)	Management of human capital
11-01	Put procedures in place to periodically monitor the effectiveness of the new First-time Homebuyer Credit (FTHBC) validity checks for the duration of the filing of FTHBC claims to verify that they are working as intended. (short-term)	Reviews by management at the functional or activity level
11-02	Establish a mechanism to enforce the existing requirement for appropriate managers to immediately notify the manual refund units of any personnel changes affecting the approval or processing of manual refunds. This may be accomplished through mechanisms such as issuing periodic alerts, providing training or having the manual refund unit perform quarterly validations of the list of manual refund approving officials, or a combination of these. (short-term)	Reviews by management at the functional or activity level

Source: GAO.

---

[3]GAO-12-165.

[4]GAO, *Management Report: Improvements Are Needed to Enhance IRS's Internal Controls and Operating Effectiveness*, GAO-11-494R (Washington, D.C.: June 21, 2011); *Management Report: Improvements Needed in IRS's Internal Controls*, GAO-07-689R (Washington, D.C.: May 11, 2007); *Management Report: Improvements Needed in IRS's Internal Controls*, GAO-06-543R (Washington, D.C.: May 12, 2006); and *Management Report: Improvements Needed in IRS's Internal Controls*, GAO-05-247R (Washington, D.C.: Apr. 27, 2005).

Compliance with Laws and Regulations: Release of Federal Tax Liens

IRS continues to be noncompliant with the laws and regulations governing the release of federal tax liens.[5] We found IRS did not always release applicable federal tax liens within 30 days of tax liabilities being either paid off or abated, as required by the Internal Revenue Code (section 6325). The Internal Revenue Code grants IRS the power to file a lien against the property of any taxpayer who neglects or refuses to pay all assessed federal taxes. The lien serves to protect the interest of the federal government and as a public notice to current and potential creditors of the federal government's interest in the taxpayer's property. The recommendation in table 14 addresses our related finding.

Table 14: Compliance with Laws and Regulations: Release of Federal Tax Liens

ID no.	Recommendation	Control activity
01-06	Implement procedures to closely monitor the release of tax liens to ensure that they are released within 30 days of the date the related tax liability is fully satisfied. As part of these procedures, IRS should carefully analyze the causes of the delays in releasing tax liens identified by our work and prior work by IRS's former internal audit function and ensure that such procedures effectively address these issues. (short-term)	Reviews by management at the functional or activity level

Source: GAO.

Other Control Deficiencies

IRS's actions over the years to resolve control deficiencies enabled us to close over 300 internal control–related recommendations. However, IRS also continues to face a challenge in addressing numerous other unresolved control deficiencies in several aspects of its operations that, while neither individually nor collectively representing a material weakness or significant deficiency, nonetheless merit management attention to ensure they are fully and effectively addressed. IRS now has a total of 57 open audit recommendations resulting from control deficiencies that we report in table 15. While most were identified during our recent financial audits, some were identified in our audits since 2005. It is incumbent upon IRS to effectively address these open recommendations and to improve its system of internal controls so that IRS can identify and correct potential control deficiencies before they can grow into more serious problems.

Twenty-five —over 40 percent—of the 57 "other" open recommendations address control deficiencies related either directly or indirectly to physical

---

[5]GAO-12-165.

safeguarding of tax receipts and taxpayer information, a critical element of IRS's responsibilities.[6]

IRS processes billions of dollars annually in checks and currency, which it must safeguard and account for to prevent theft, fraud, and misuse. To do so, IRS has established physical security, accountability, and accounting policies, processes, and procedures to manage its activities involving transporting and accounting for tax receipts and for handling and storing taxpayer information. Although IRS has made substantial improvements in safeguarding taxpayer receipts and information since our financial audits first began identifying serious control deficiencies in this area, the task of ensuring ongoing control over such critical responsibilities for IRS is a difficult one and requires constant vigilance. Each year, we continue to identify control deficiencies related to IRS's safeguarding of taxpayer receipts and information. For example, our fiscal year 2011 audit identified new control deficiencies, and we made additional recommendations that related either directly or indirectly to physically safeguarding taxpayer receipts and information. The control deficiencies encompassed in our open recommendations cover critical physical security functions, such as

- transporting taxpayer receipts and sensitive taxpayer information among IRS facilities and lockbox banks[7] and maintaining physical security at IRS facilities to prevent loss, theft, or the potential for fraud regarding tax receipts and taxpayer information;

- conducting inspections and audits of the design and operation of IRS's physical security processes and controls designed to safeguard tax receipts and taxpayer information; and

---

[6]IRS's need to safeguard tax receipts and taxpayer information extends beyond the control activity of safeguarding assets, as reflected in tables 1 through 4 of this report. For our analysis in this section, we included recommendations related directly to guarding tax information and receipts, such as the transportation of information between IRS facilities, and those indirectly related, such as IRS's need to obtain background investigations on individuals with access to tax receipts or information.

[7]Lockbox banks are financial institutions designated as depositories and financial agents of the U.S. government to perform certain financial services, including processing tax documents, depositing the receipts, and forwarding the documents and data to the IRS service center campuses (SCC) that process tax returns and payments.

- conducting appropriate background investigations and screening of personnel, including contractors, with access to taxpayer information.

In light of the volume of taxpayer receipts and sensitive taxpayer files that IRS is responsible for safeguarding, and the implications for IRS's mission if they are lost, stolen, or the subject of fraud or misuse, it is critical that IRS fully and effectively resolve the control deficiencies we have identified and work toward continually improving its internal controls to prevent new issues from arising.

Table 15: Other Control Deficiencies Not Associated with a Material Weakness, Significant Deficiency, or Compliance Issue

ID no.	Recommendation	Control activity
05-33	Enforce the requirement that a document transmittal form listing the enclosed Daily Report of Collection Activity forms be included in transmittal packages, using such methods as more frequent inspections or increased reliance on error reports compiled by the service center teller units receiving the information. (short-term)	Reviews by management at the functional or activity level
06-02	Enforce compliance with existing requirements that all IRS units transmitting taxpayer receipts and information from one IRS facility to another, including service center campuses (SCC), Taxpayer Assistance Centers (TAC), and units within the Large Business and International (LB&I) and the Tax-Exempt and Government Entities (TE/GE) business operating units, establish a system to track acknowledged copies of document transmittals. (short-term)	Appropriate documentation of transactions and internal controls
06-05	Equip all TACs with adequate physical security controls to deter and prevent unauthorized access to restricted areas or office space occupied by other IRS units, including those TACs that are not scheduled to be reconfigured to the "new TAC" model in the near future. This includes appropriately separating customer service waiting areas from restricted areas in the near future by physical barriers, such as locked doors marked with signs barring entrance by unescorted customers. (short-term)	Physical control over vulnerable assets
07-04	Develop and implement appropriate corrective actions for any gaps in closed circuit television (CCTV) camera coverage that do not provide an unobstructed view of the entire exterior of the SCC perimeter, such as adding or repositioning existing CCTV cameras or removing obstructions. (short-term)	Physical control over vulnerable assets
08-14	Revise the Internal Revenue Manual (IRM) to include a requirement that IRS conduct periodic, unannounced inspections at off-site contractor facilities entrusted with sensitive IRS information; document the results, including identification of any security issues; and verify that the contractor has taken appropriate corrective actions on any security issues observed. (short-term)	Reviews by management at the functional or activity level
09-03	Document in the IRM minimum requirements for establishing criteria for time discrepancies or other inconsistencies, which if noted as part of the required monitoring of Form 10160, Receipt for Transport of IRS Deposit, would require off-site surveillance of couriers. (short-term)	Physical control over vulnerable assets
09-05	Establish procedures to track and routinely report the total dollar amounts and volumes of receipts collected by individual TAC location, group, territory, area, and nationwide. (long-term)	Reviews by management at the functional or activity level
09-06	Establish procedures to ensure that an inventory of all duress alarms is documented for each location and is readily available to individuals conducting duress alarm tests before each test is conducted. (short-term)	Physical control over vulnerable assets

ID no.	Recommendation	Control activity
09-07	Establish procedures to periodically update the inventory of duress alarms at each TAC location to ensure that the inventory is current and complete as of the testing date. (short-term)	Physical control over vulnerable assets
09-08	Provide instructions for conducting quarterly duress alarm tests to ensure that IRS officials conducting the test (1) document the test results for each duress alarm listed in the inventory, including date, findings, and planned corrective action and (2) track the findings until they are properly resolved. (short-term)	Physical control over vulnerable assets
09-09	Establish procedures requiring that each physical security analyst conduct a periodic documented review of the Emergency Signal History Report and emergency contact list for its respective location to ensure that (1) appropriate corrective actions have been planned for all incidents reported by the central monitoring station and (2) the emergency contact list for each location is current and includes only appropriate contacts. (short-term)	Physical control over vulnerable assets
09-16	Develop outcome-oriented performance measures and related performance goals for IRS's enforcement programs and activities that include measures of the full cost of, and the revenue collected from, those programs and activities (return on investment) to assist IRS's managers in optimizing resource allocation decisions and evaluating the effectiveness of their activities. (long-term)	Establishment and review of performance measures and indicators
10-19	Establish procedures to track service center campus (SCC) acknowledgments of unprocessable items with receipts. (short-term)	Physical control over vulnerable assets
10-20	Establish procedures to monitor the process used by service center campuses (SCC) and lockbox banks to acknowledge and track transmittals of unprocessable items with receipts. These procedures should include monitoring discrepancies and instituting appropriate corrective actions as needed. (short-term)	Physical control over vulnerable assets
10-29	Analyze the various contractor access arrangements and establish a policy that requires security awareness training for all IRS contractors who are provided unescorted physical access to its facilities or taxpayer receipts and information. (short-term)	Access restrictions to and accountability for resources and records
11-04	Establish formal written procedures requiring staff to review purchase contract terms against the goods and services received to date before requesting additional goods or services (short-term)	Accurate and timely recording of transactions and events
11-05	Establish procedures to centrally review and monitor the timeliness of personnel action requests and approvals to help ensure compliance with the IRM and applicable Office of Personnel Management (OPM) regulations and guidance. (short-term)	Accurate and timely recording of transactions and events
11-11	Perform a review of all existing contracts under $100,000 that (1) do not have an appointed contracting officer's technical representative (COTR) and (2) do not require that contract employees obtain background investigations to assess whether the services performed under each contract warrant a requirement that contract employees obtain background investigations. (short-term)	Access restrictions to and accountability for resources and records
11-12	Based on a review of all existing contracts under $100,000 without an appointed COTR that should require contract employees to obtain favorable background investigation results, amend those contracts to require that favorable background investigations be obtained for all relevant contract employees before routine, unescorted, unsupervised physical access to taxpayer information is granted. (short-term)	Access restrictions to and accountability for resources and records

GAO-12-695 Status of Recommendations

ID no.	Recommendation	Control activity
11-13	Establish a policy requiring collaborative oversight between IRS's key offices in determining whether potential service contracts involve routine, unescorted, unsupervised physical access to taxpayer information, thus requiring background investigations, regardless of contract award amount. This policy should include a process for the requiring business unit to communicate to the Office of Procurement and the Human Capital Office the services to be provided under the contract and any potential exposure of taxpayer information to contract employees providing the services, and for all three units to (1) evaluate the risk of exposure of taxpayer information prior to finalizing and awarding the contract and (2) ensure that the final contract requires favorable background investigations as applicable, commensurate with the assessed risk. (short-term)	Access restrictions to and accountability for resources and records
11-14	Establish procedures to provide a consistent methodology for calculating and establishing allowable deposit courier trip time limits to be used by both service center campuses (SCC) and lockbox banks that would assist in detecting potential unauthorized stops or other contractual violations by deposit couriers. Such procedures should include instructions for documenting and supporting how the trip limits were determined and require justification and approval for all established time limits that exceed the average trip time. (short-term)	Physical control over vulnerable assets
11-16	Enforce existing contractual requirements for the cargo doors of contract courier vehicles to be locked after picking up taxpayer information. (short-term)	Physical control over vulnerable assets
11-17	Establish procedures to prevent or detect unauthorized access to taxpayer information in contract courier vehicles during transit. These procedures should detail specific activities to be performed by both the business unit sending and receiving the information transported by the contract courier. (short-term)	Physical control over vulnerable assets
11-18	Revise the guidance for conducting the periodic reviews of the contract couriers transporting taxpayer information from one IRS processing facility to another to include procedures for (1) physically verifying that courier vehicle cargo doors are locked after picking up this information and remain locked during transit to the final destination and (2) documenting the basis for the reviewer's conclusions. (short-term)	Physical control over vulnerable assets
11-24	Revise the post orders for the SCC and lockbox bank security guards to include specific procedures for timely reporting exterior lighting outages to SCC or lockbox bank facilities management. These procedures should specify (1) whom to contact to report lighting outages and (2) how to document and track lighting outages until resolved. (short-term)	Appropriate documentation of transactions and internal controls
11-25	Revise the nature and scope of the SCC and lockbox banks' physical security reviews to include periodic after dark assessments of physical security controls. (short-term)	Reviews by management at the functional or activity level
11-26	Take steps to effectively implement the procedures requiring property staff to verify that the asset purchase price shown in the Asset Management Report agrees with the asset purchase price shown in the Integrated Financial System (IFS) and to resolve any variances before entering the information into the Information Technology Asset Management System (ITAMS). (short-term)	Accurate and timely recording of transactions and events
12-01	Establish and document an inventory of the specific systems involved in IRS's financial reporting process, including (1) describing what role each system plays in the financial reporting process, (2) concluding whether each system is considered to be material to financial reporting and why, and (3) denoting whether each system is controlled by IRS or by an external service provider and, if the latter, identifying the service provider. (short-term)	Reviews by management at the functional or activity level

GAO-12-695 Status of Recommendations

ID no.	Recommendation	Control activity
12-02	Enhance existing policies and procedures pertaining to monitoring internal control over the automated systems operated by IRS personnel to specifically provide for routine, documented monitoring of the specific internal controls within its financial reporting systems that are intended to ensure the integrity of the data reported in the financial statements and other financial reports. This monitoring process should (1) involve both automated systems specialists and individuals with expertise in accounting and reporting, as appropriate, (2) encompass the specific automated internal controls that affect the authorizing, processing, transmitting, or reporting of material financial transactions, and (3) be designed to determine whether these internal controls are in place and operating effectively. (short-term)	Reviews by management at the functional or activity level
12-03	For any system identified as material to IRS's financial reporting process which is controlled by an external service provider, establish policies and procedures requiring and defining a routine, documented process for coordinating with the service provider to appropriately monitor related internal control. This may entail establishing an agreement with each service provider to allow IRS personnel the access to either (1) the system concerned, as necessary to perform appropriate monitoring of internal control over financial reporting, or (2) periodic reports prepared in accordance with Statements on Standards for Attestation Engagements (SSAE) No. 16 documenting the results of monitoring performed by the service provider. (short-term)	Reviews by management at the functional or activity level
12-04	Establish policies and procedures with respect to any external financial reporting system IRS personnel themselves do not directly monitor that specify required steps to routinely review periodic reports prepared by service providers' auditors in accordance with SSAE No. 16, including steps to document (1) an assessment of whether a review's scope, methodology, and timing is appropriate to satisfy IRS's objectives; (2) any control deficiencies disclosed in the report, and an assessment of their materiality to IRS's financial reporting process and related risks; and (3) any compensating internal controls needed to mitigate any actual or potential effects of identified deficiencies upon IRS's internal and external financial reports resulting from any (a) material weakness, or (b) significant shortcoming in the scope, methodology, or timing of any SSAE No. 16 report reviewed relative to IRS's internal control objectives. (short-term)	Reviews by management at the functional or activity level
12-05	Update IRS's procedures for comparing tax revenue recorded in the general ledger to detailed tax revenue transactions recorded in the master files to (1) establish minimum criteria defining a significant or unusual variance and (2) specify the steps required to effectively evaluate and resolve these variances. (short-term)	Appropriate documentation of transactions and internal controls
12-06	Update IRS's procedures for comparing tax revenue recorded in the general ledger to detailed tax revenue transactions recorded in the master files to require that management reviews ensure preparers evaluate and resolve unusual or significant variances. (short-term)	Appropriate documentation of transactions and internal controls
12-07	Establish and document procedures for ensuring that recorded reimbursable revenue, transfers in without reimbursement, and accounts receivable from the Department of the Treasury Forfeiture Fund (TFF) conform to federal accounting standards. (short-term)	Accurate and timely recording of transactions and events
12-08	Establish requirements specifying a required time frame for territory managers to perform the required review and approval of completed audit management checklists. (short-term)	Reviews by management at the functional or activity level
12-09	Establish procedures requiring Physical Security and Emergency Preparedness (PSEP) headquarters to centrally monitor compliance with the audit management checklist process to ensure that (1) PSEP analysts timely complete their physical security reviews using the proper audit management checklists and (2) territory managers timely review and properly document their reviews of completed audit management checklists. (short-term)	Reviews by management at the functional or activity level

ID no.	Recommendation	Control activity
12-10	Update the IRM to specify steps to be followed to prevent campus support clerks as well as any other employees who process payments through the electronic check presentment system from making adjustments to taxpayer accounts. (short-term)	Segregation of duties
12-11	Implement the September 2011 revised policy that requires an independent review of the rent check summary report to help ensure that the monthly rent allocation process is properly completed. (short-term)	Reviews by management at the functional or activity level
12-12	Establish a policy requiring an independent review of changes made by the rent processing administrator to non-GSA lease data in the Graphic Database Interface system (GDI). (short-term)	Reviews by management at the functional or activity level
12-13	Revise existing written procedures to require supervisory review of the Computer-Aided Facilities Management (CAFM) Quarterly Review Certifications and Statistics against the GDI validation walkthrough sheets. (short-term)	Appropriate documentation of transactions and internal controls
12-14	Establish mechanisms to monitor the implementation of and compliance with the revised policy established in October 2011 that requires field Computer-Aided Facilities Management (CAFM) program managers to maintain GDI Quarterly Review documentation, including GDI validation walkthrough sheets and GDI Quarterly Review certifications. (short-term)	Appropriate documentation of transactions and internal controls
12-15	Establish mechanisms to monitor the implementation of and compliance with the revised policy established in October 2011 that defines the type of errors that should be captured on the CAFM Quarterly Review Certifications to help ensure that field CAFM program managers consistently compile the errors found in their quarterly reviews for compilation in the overall CAFM Quarterly Review Statistics. (short-term)	Appropriate documentation of transactions and internal controls
12-16	Establish procedures to require the Office of Financial Reporting to ensure that extracted GDI data used to calculate the leasehold improvement disposal estimate is complete and accurate. (short-term)	Accurate and timely recording of transactions and events
12-17	Implement the revised January 2012 procedures requiring comparison of the leases used in the prior year with the current year leases to help ensure that expired leases have not been extended and thus, are only counted once in the disposal estimates. (short-term)	Proper execution of transactions and events
12-18	Implement the revised January 2012 procedures requiring preparation and review of leasehold improvement disposal calculations quarterly. (short-term)	Proper execution of transactions and events
12-19	Provide training to contracting officers and contracting officers' technical representatives (COTR) on their specific procedural requirements for obtaining and maintaining end user documentation of receipt and acceptance of the good or service prior to entering acknowledgment of receipt and acceptance in the procurement system. (short-term)	Management of human capital
12-20	Establish a mechanism to periodically monitor contracting officers and contracting officers' technical representatives (COTR) compliance with the requirement to obtain and document end user confirmation of receipt prior to entering receipt and acceptance into the procurement system. (short-term)	Accurate and timely recording of transactions and events
12-21	Establish a mechanism for monitoring compliance with the existing requirement for employees and timekeepers to charge labor time spent on the Patient Protection and Affordable Care Act (PPACA) projects to the PPACA accounting code, such as through issuing periodic alerts, providing training and guidance, and/or having managers perform periodic reviews of employee labor time charges. (short-term)	Accurate and timely recording of transactions and events
12-22	Design and implement procedures specifying the review steps required to identify and research all transactions identified with a PPACA internal order number in the agency's expense files to confirm that they are PPACA-related expenses and, if so, to ensure that they are charged to the PPACA appropriation where appropriate. (short-term)	Accurate and timely recording of transactions and events

ID no.	Recommendation	Control activity
12-23	Revise the payroll standard operating procedures to specify steps that the human resource specialists are required to follow to ensure that each electronic time card is signed by an authorized official before the timecard is transmitted to the National Finance Center for processing and payment. (short-term)	Proper execution of transactions and events
12-24	Revise the payroll standard operating procedures to require that the designated proxy for a manager required to approve time cards be at an equivalent or higher level as the manager, consistent with the IRM. (short-term)	Proper execution of transactions and events
12-25	Incorporate in the planned 2012 policy change requiring the manager or designated proxy to sign the electronic time card before transmitting payroll records to the National Finance Center the requirement that the designated proxy be at an equivalent or higher level than the employee's manager. (short-term)	Proper execution of transactions and events
12-26	Implement an edit control in IRS's time card system to identify and prevent the processing of time cards that have not been electronically signed. (short-term)	Accurate and timely recording of transactions and events
12-27	Remind managers of their responsibilities, procedures, and required time frames for either granting or denying a within-grade pay increase for employees with below fully successful ratings, such as by providing alerts in HR Connect when a manager enters a less than fully successful rating or providing training to remind them of their responsibilities. (short-term)	Management of human capital
12-28	Establish procedures for human resource specialists to track and monitor supervisory actions taken for employees with less than fully successful ratings that have a within-grade pay increase due date within 90 days to include specific required steps for following-up with managers to ensure the managers properly issue the employees a 60-day notification letter providing them an opportunity to improve their performance, make a timely determination on releasing or denying a within-grade pay increase, and properly carry out the requirements necessary to support the decision made. (short-term)	Reviews by management at the functional or activity level
12-29	Establish procedures for HR specialists to track and monitor supervisory actions taken for employees with less than fully successful ratings that have a within-grade pay increase due date within 90 days to include specific required steps for timely granting a within-grade pay increase to such employees who were not given a 60-day notification letter. (short-term)	Reviews by management at the functional or activity level
12-30	Establish and document procedures for payroll staff to research and correct recycled errors from payroll processing on a regular and timely basis. (short-term)	Accurate and timely recording of transactions and events

Source: GAO.

Appendix III: Comments from the Internal Revenue Service

DEPARTMENT OF THE TREASURY
INTERNAL REVENUE SERVICE
WASHINGTON, D.C. 20224

COMMISSIONER

June 18, 2012

Mr. Steven J. Sebastian
Managing Director
Financial Management and Assurance
U.S. Government Accountability Office
441 G Street, NW
Washington, DC 20548

Dear Mr. Sebastian:

I am writing in response to the Government Accountability Office (GAO) draft report titled *IRS: Status of GAO Financial Audit and Related Financial Management Recommendations (GAO-12-695).*

As GAO noted in the report, IRS has made significant progress in improving its internal controls and financial management as evidenced by 12 consecutive years of clean audit opinions on its financial statement. We are pleased that you acknowledged our progress in addressing our financial management challenges and agreed to close 38 prior year financial management recommendations.

We are committed to implementing appropriate improvements to ensure that the IRS maintains sound financial management practices. If you have any questions, please contact me, or a member of your staff may contact Pamela LaRue, Chief Financial Officer, at (202) 622-6400.

Sincerely,

Douglas H. Shulman

Appendix IV: GAO Contact and Staff Acknowledgments

GAO Contact	Steven J. Sebastian, (202) 512-3406 or sebastians@gao.gov
Staff Acknowledgments	In addition to the contact named above, the following individuals made major contributions to this report: William J. Cordrey, Assistant Director; Crystal Alfred; Ray B. Bush; Sunny Chang; Stephanie Chen; Jeremy Choi; Nina Crocker; Doreen Eng; Charles Fox; Ted Hu; Tuan Lam; Delores Lee; Jenny Li; Cynthia Ma; Joshua Marcus; Marc Oestreicher; Julie Phillips; James Rinaldi; John Sawyer; Christopher Spain; Cynthia Tedd eton; Lien To; LaDonna Towler; Cherry Vasquez; and Gary Wiggins.

GAO's Mission	The Government Accountability Office, the audit, evaluation, and investigative arm of Congress, exists to support Congress in meeting its constitutional responsibilities and to help improve the performance and accountability of the federal government for the American people. GAO examines the use of public funds; evaluates federal programs and policies; and provides analyses, recommendations, and other assistance to help Congress make informed oversight, policy, and funding decisions. GAO's commitment to good government is reflected in its core values of accountability, integrity, and reliability.
Obtaining Copies of GAO Reports and Testimony	The fastest and easiest way to obtain copies of GAO documents at no cost is through GAO's website (www.gao.gov). Each weekday afternoon, GAO posts on its website newly released reports, testimony, and correspondence. To have GAO e-mail you a list of newly posted products, go to www.gao.gov and select "E-mail Updates."
Order by Phone	The price of each GAO publication reflects GAO's actual cost of production and distribution and depends on the number of pages in the publication and whether the publication is printed in color or black and white. Pricing and ordering information is posted on GAO's website, http://www.gao.gov/ordering.htm.
	Place orders by calling (202) 512-6000, toll free (866) 801-7077, or TDD (202) 512-2537.
	Orders may be paid for using American Express, Discover Card, MasterCard, Visa, check, or money order. Call for additional information.
Connect with GAO	Connect with GAO on Facebook, Flickr, Twitter, and YouTube. Subscribe to our RSS Feeds or E-mail Updates. Listen to our Podcasts. Visit GAO on the web at www.gao.gov.
To Report Fraud, Waste, and Abuse in Federal Programs	Contact: Website: www.gao.gov/fraudnet/fraudnet.htm E-mail: fraudnet@gao.gov Automated answering system: (800) 424-5454 or (202) 512-7470
Congressional Relations	Katherine Siggerud, Managing Director, siggerudk@gao.gov, (202) 512-4400, U.S. Government Accountability Office, 441 G Street NW, Room 7125, Washington, DC 20548
Public Affairs	Chuck Young, Managing Director, youngc1@gao.gov, (202) 512-4800 U.S. Government Accountability Office, 441 G Street NW, Room 7149 Washington, DC 20548

Please Print on Recycled Paper.